Solar Cooking Naturally

by Virginia Heather Gurley

by Virginia Heather Gurley

ISBN: 0-9634694-4-4

Publisher: SunLightWorks

P.O. Box 3386 • Sedona • Arizona • 86340
(602) 282-1202

Cover design and illustrations by Annie Fisher

Printed on recycled paper
in gratitude for the trees.

Printed in the United States of America

May the Joy of
Solar Cooking
Be Yours to
Share.

ORGANIZATIONS PROMOTING SOLAR COOKING

Brace Research Institute
P.O. Box 900, McGille University, St. Anne de
Bellevue, Quebec, Canada H9X 1C0

Children's Earth Fund
40 W. 20th St., New York, NY 10011 USA

Committee for the National Institutes of Environment
730 11th St. NW, Washington, DC 20001 USA

Communities In Partnership
6833 Cranberry St., Powell River, B.C.
V0N 2G0 Canada

Dept. of Non-Conventional Energy
A1-18, Sector 11, Purania Crossing Aliganj
Lucknow, 226020 India

EG-Solar Atotting
Karl Valentine St. 20, 8265 Neuotting, Germany

GATE • P.O. Box 5180, D-6236, Eschborn 1, Germany

Gruppe ULOG
Morgartenring 18, CH-4054, Basel, Switzerland

Islamic African Relief Agency
P.O. Box 7084, Columbia, MO 65205 USA

Renewable Energy Training Institute
122 C Street, NW Suite 520, Washington, DC
20001 USA

SERVE • Box 477, Peshawar, Pakistan

Sacramento Municipal Utility District (SMUD)
P.O. Box 15830, Sacramento, CA 95852-1830 USA

Solar Box Cookers International *Quarterly Newsletter*
1724 Eleventh St., Sacramento, CA 95814 USA

Solar Box Cookers Northwest *Solar Box Journal*
7036 18th Avenue, NE, Seattle, WA 98115 USA

Solar Energy International
P.O. Box 1115, Carbondale, CO 81623 USA

Synopsis • Route d'Olmet, F34700 Lodeve, France

World Nature Conservation Mission
P.O. Box Section, Calapan, Or Mindoro,
Philippines 5200

WorldWide • 1331 H St., NW, Washington, DC 20005 USA

World Association Girl Guides / Girl Scouts
3523 Rolph Way, El Dorado Hills, CA 95630 USA

TABLE OF CONTENTS

All recipes in this book have been tested using a solar oven. If you don't have a solar oven yet, you can simply set your conventional oven at 325°F (97° C) and enjoy success.

INTRODUCTION

Solar cooking is a whole, new, fresh approach to cooked foods. The sun is the primary and crucial source of light to the planet. Without the sun there would be no life. When sunlight is trapped in a solar oven, food cooks by natural light transformed into heat energy. This event is simple to apply and understand. It is called **Solar Cooking Naturally.**

Solar cooking is superior to dry heat methods of conventional gas and electric stoves. Solar cooking also offers an ecological alternative to using firewood for cooking food. It is the vital rays of the sun which cook the food at slow, low temperatures. The essential juices of each vegetable or meat are retained by the live dynamics of sun cooking. Solar cooking requires new definition in the culinary world. "Nutritional physics" is the term given to express the quality of solar cooked, energized food.

ADVANTAGES OF SOLAR COOKING

Solar cooking offers a wide range of advantages. Enjoy energy self-sufficiency with a solar oven. Indeed, it is a convenient solar cooking appliance.

1. The solar oven uses free energy.

2. The sun energizes cooked food with natural heat energy. The food is a gourmet tasting experience.

3. The sun's energy is safe, non-polluting and an abundant renewable energy source.

4. You can lower utility bills by 10-15% when a solar oven is used consistently.

5. Baking with the sun takes the heat out of the house in the summer.

6. A solar oven can be used to can fruit and make fruit leather.

7. Solar cooking is nutritionally sound. It is almost waterless cooking, thus vitamins and minerals are retained in the juices of the vegetables and meats.

8. Solar cooking is a joy filled art. Cooking times do not have to be specific. The food cooks slowly, needing little monitoring.

SOLAR COOKERS:
A GLOBAL SOLUTION

Cooking with solar energy can make a major contribution to the management of many global problems.

Problem: In many parts of the world, wood is the primary cooking fuel. Using wood fuel for cooking has contributed to large scale deforestation. Every day 1 million tons of wood are burned for cooking, the rough equivalent of 100 square kilometers of forest.

Solution: Solar cooking is an efficient way to relieve deforestation in regions where firewood is widely used for cooking.

Problem: Emergency and disaster relief cannot rely on conventional forms of energy.

Solution: Solar cookers can save lives when electricity, gas or wood supplies are disrupted. The solar cooker is a survival tool. Solar ovens can even be used to disinfect medical instruments.

Problem: The World Health Organization estimates that about 50,000 people die everyday from diseases associated with contaminated drinking water. This is a critical problem for large portions of the world's population.

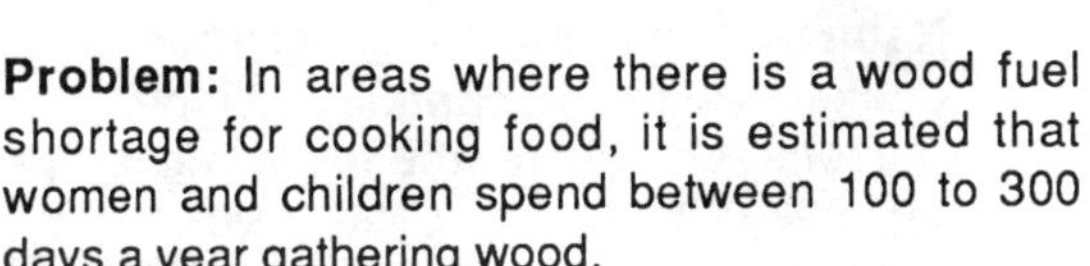

Solution: Solar cookers can pasteurize water through simple methods of heating water past 65C• or 150 F².

Problem: In areas where there is a wood fuel shortage for cooking food, it is estimated that women and children spend between 100 to 300 days a year gathering wood.

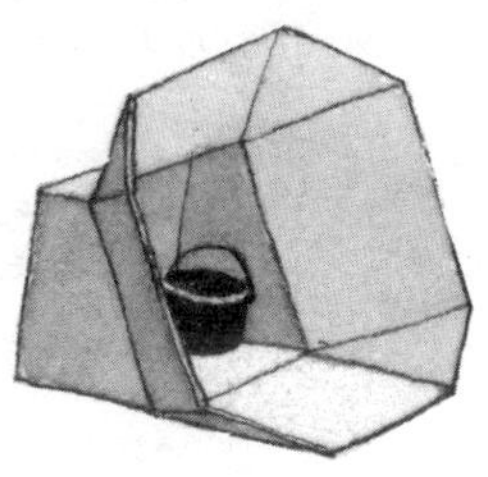

Solution: Solar cooking frees up women's time for greater contributions to family, economics and health needs. Children can spend more time attending school. Solar cooking is easily taught to school age children.

There are many innovations in solar cooker designs. The illustration on these pages depict a few examples of solar cooking technologies being used around the world. To learn more about organizations who are directing their efforts to promoting this valuable tool, refer to Appendix One.

COOKING TIPS

There is no secret to the art of solar cooking. The most basic ingredient is the available sunlight in your area on a given day. It is usually advisable to pre-heat your solar oven before starting to cook. It will take approximately 20-45 minutes for the oven to warm up depending on the season of the year. Preferred cookware is any dark pot with a lid. A light color will reflect light back out of the cooker. The Kerr-Cole Eco-Cooker II is the solar oven chosen to test and time the recipes for Solar Cooking Naturally. In addition to its roominess, this cooker is within economic availability for most persons. Of course, the following recipes can be used with any solar cooker including backyard projects of your own design. Simple to use, the following are a few tips for successful cookery in a Kerr-Cole oven.

1. A cake rack under the pan allows heat to circulate and cook evenly.
2. Mid-day baking is best for bread and cakes.
3. When it rains cover your oven and use your emergency backup — a standard electric, gas, wooden or microwave range.

4. The solar oven can defrost and then cook frozen breads, casseroles and roasts.

5. On clear sunny days the oven will heat up between 250-300 degrees. You can bake and cook just about anything on these days.

6 . With partly cloudy or polluted skies, the oven ranges between 200-250 degrees. You can cook meat, rice, potatoes, warm up leftovers and prepare egg dishes.

7 . The frequency of re-focusing the cooker towards the sun depends on what is cooking and your schedule. To keep maximum heat adjust every 30 minutes.

8. Passive and absentee cooking means setting the oven and reflector to suit your schedule. In the morning, a working person can set an oven at noon (directly south) with a pot roast and return hours later with dinner hot, but unburned.

9. Use pot holders and don't get burned when taking food out of the oven.

10. Pre-heated water will shorten cooking time.

11. When cooking a grain you may consider making more for the next day's soup or casserole.

12. Spaghetti pasta can be solar cooked by heating up the water and the dry pasta in separate containers for at least one hour, then combining them, quickly stirring, covering and cooking for 1/2 - 3/4 hour or longer. Try it! It works!

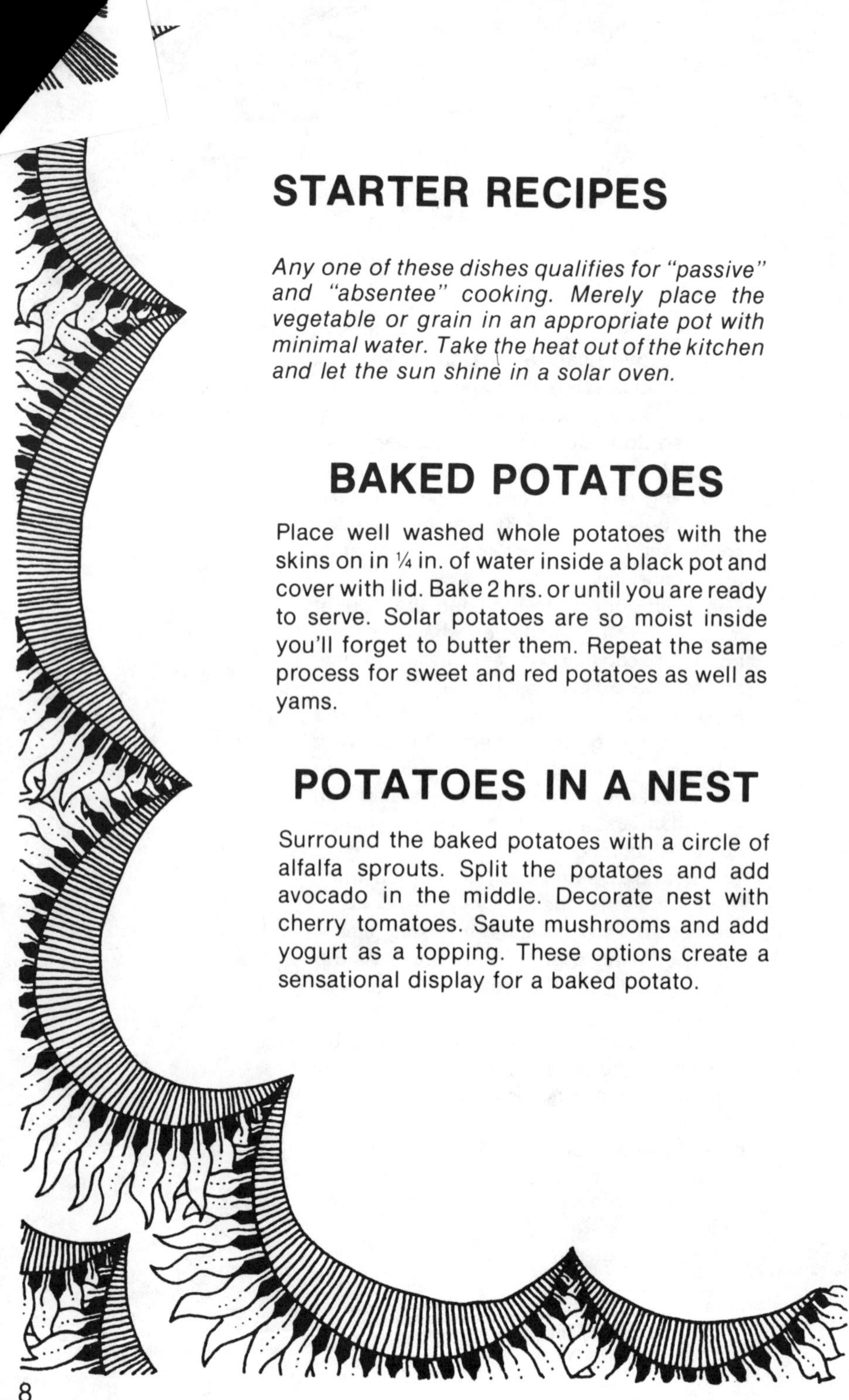

STARTER RECIPES

Any one of these dishes qualifies for "passive" and "absentee" cooking. Merely place the vegetable or grain in an appropriate pot with minimal water. Take the heat out of the kitchen and let the sun shine in a solar oven.

BAKED POTATOES

Place well washed whole potatoes with the skins on in ¼ in. of water inside a black pot and cover with lid. Bake 2 hrs. or until you are ready to serve. Solar potatoes are so moist inside you'll forget to butter them. Repeat the same process for sweet and red potatoes as well as yams.

POTATOES IN A NEST

Surround the baked potatoes with a circle of alfalfa sprouts. Split the potatoes and add avocado in the middle. Decorate nest with cherry tomatoes. Saute mushrooms and add yogurt as a topping. These options create a sensational display for a baked potato.

SQUASH

The family of winter squash varieties, including spaghetti squash, presents a simple, economical nourishing meal. The squash can be cooked whole. Place it in one-half inch of water inside a black pot and cover. Bake until tender, depending on size, amount in pot and variety of squash--usually 3 hours.

EASY GRANOLA

This ingenious recipe hails from Barbara Kerr, inventor of the Eco Cooker solar box cooker.

1 c. each raw oat, rye and barley flakes
1/2 c. honey
1/2 c. nut butter, melted
optional dry fruits or nuts

Spread mixture thin on cookie trays. Stir each hour. Bake until crisp.

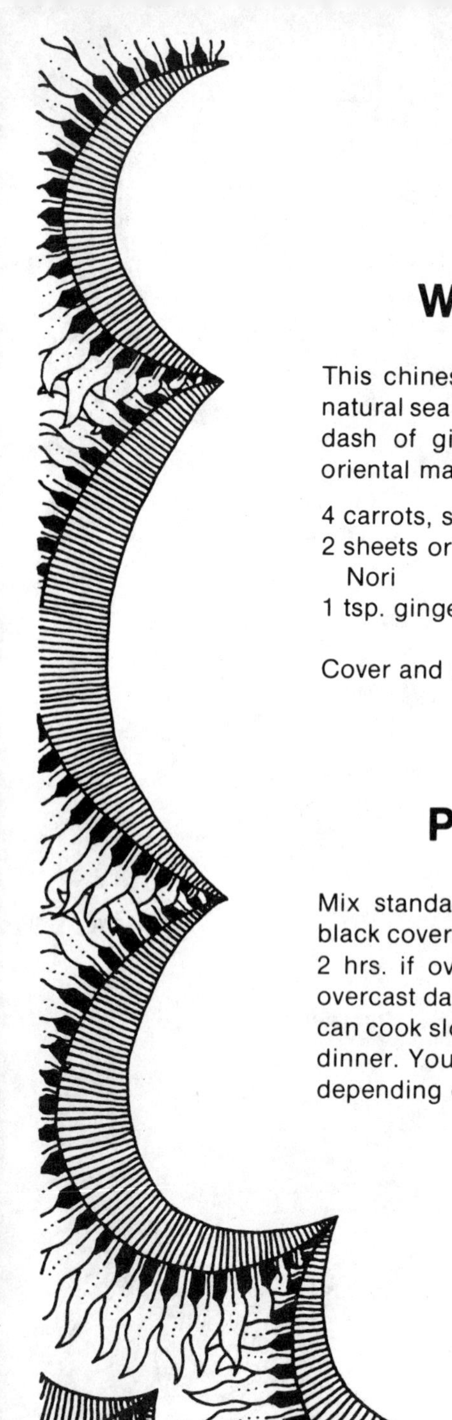

CARROTS WITH SEAWEED

This chinese-like dish is full of minerals and natural sea salt when baked with seaweed. The dash of ginger and tamari/soy sauce adds oriental magic.

4 carrots, sliced
2 sheets or strips of
   Nori
1 tsp. ginger

3 tbs. tamari/soy sauce
Water to cover ¼ in.
   of pot

Cover and bake two hours.

PERFECT RICE

Mix standard amounts of rice and water in black covered pot. Place in preheated oven for 2 hrs. if oven temperature is over 250°. On overcast days when the oven is cooler the rice can cook slowly, up to 6 hrs. and be perfect for dinner. You can optionally preheat the water, depending on sky conditions.

GOLDEN MILLET

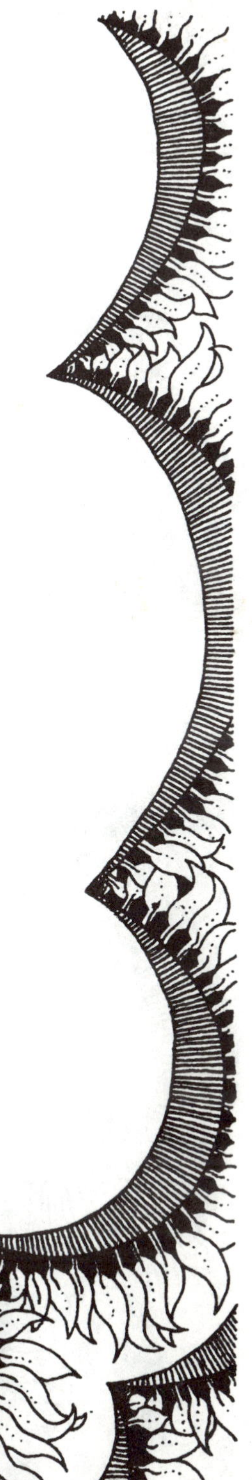

Baked millet provides low-gluten protein, calcium and lecithin. It can be used in soups, casseroles, or creamed into a hot cereal. It can replace rice in almost any recipe.

1 c. millet
2 c. water

Place in black pot and cover. Cooks in 2 hrs. On overcast days let millet bake all day.

DINNER MILLET

1 c. millet   ½ c. water or broth
½ c. carrots, chopped

Place in black pot and cook as in Basic Millet.

ROSEMARY RICE

Rosemary is a pungent herb and garnishes rice to accompany game dishes.

1 c. short grain brown rice
2 c. water
1 tsp. dried rosemary leaves
1 small onion diced
10 mushrooms, sliced

Place all ingredients in black pot with lid. Cook 2-4 hours depending on season of year.

PINTO BEANS

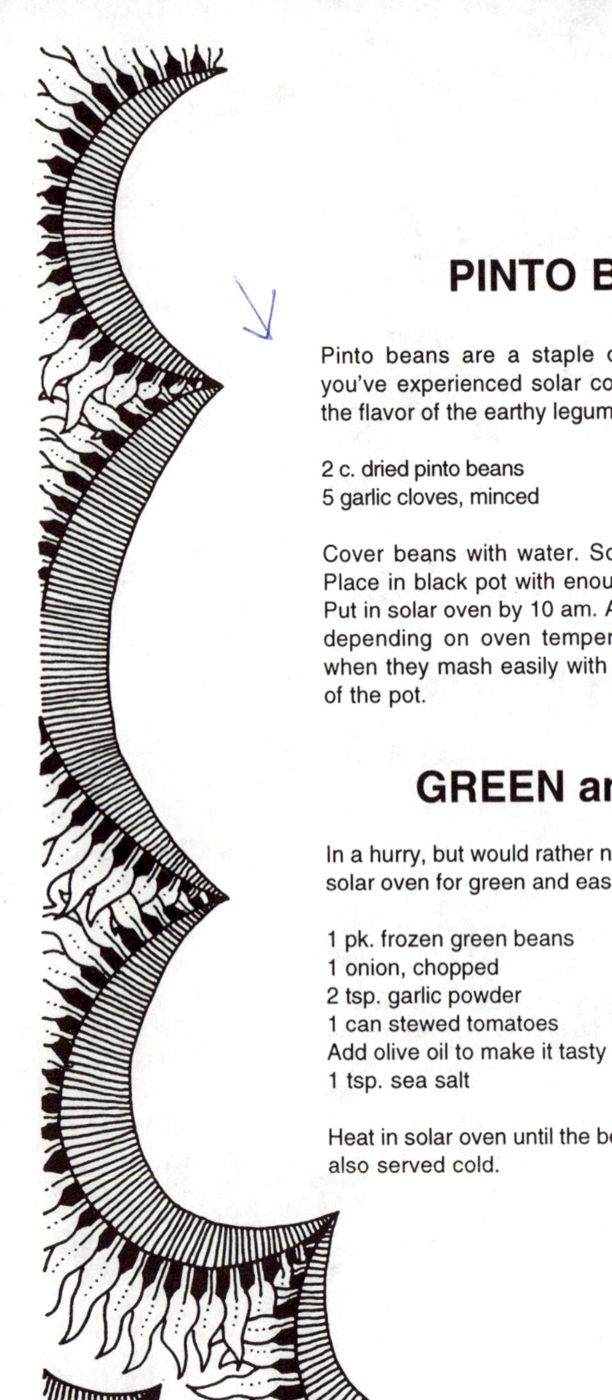

Pinto beans are a staple of the Southwest. Once you've experienced solar cooking them, you'll agree the flavor of the earthy legume is enhanced.

2 c. dried pinto beans
5 garlic cloves, minced
1 tsp. cumin
1 tsp. sea salt

Cover beans with water. Soak the beans overnight. Place in black pot with enough water and seasoning. Put in solar oven by 10 am. Allow 6-8 hrs. for cooking, depending on oven temperature. Beans are ready when they mash easily with a spoon against the side of the pot.

GREEN and EASY

In a hurry, but would rather not eat fast foods? Use a solar oven for green and easy!

1 pk. frozen green beans
1 onion, chopped
2 tsp. garlic powder
1 can stewed tomatoes
Add olive oil to make it tasty
1 tsp. sea salt

Heat in solar oven until the beans are hot. This is good also served cold.

CHEESE CRISPS

Another Southwest contribution which makes a quick lunch.

Place corn or flour tortillas on a cookie sheet. Sprinkle with grated cheese. Cook in preheated oven 10-20 minutes or until cheese melts and starts to bubble. Serve with alfalfa sprouts, or shredded spinach leaves. Top with salsa.

NACHOS con TODO

These sensational nachos include everything that makes them yummy for kids as well as adults.

Round corn chips
Grated Monterey jack cheese (amount optional)
1 16 oz. can refried beans
2 1/4 oz can black olives, diced
8 oz sour cream
Jalapeno peppers sliced to taste

Preheat the refried beans in a black pot with lid about 1 hr. When the beans are hot, layer them over the chips. Cover with the olives, jalapeno peppers, sour cream and grated cheese. Serve when the cheese has melted with your favorite salsa.

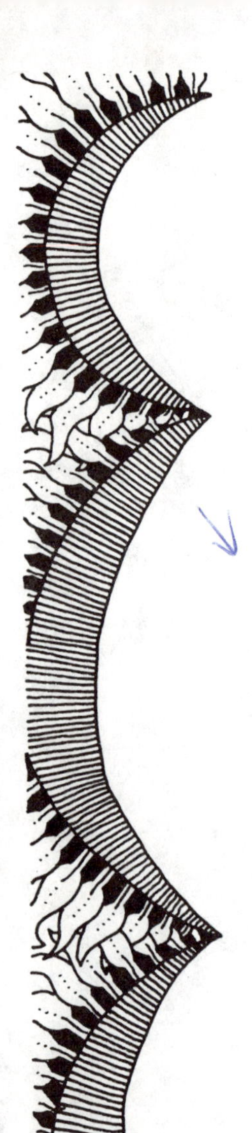

EASY EGGS

Place desired amount of eggs, covered with minimal water in oven. Eggs will hardboil in about 2 hrs. and are ready to use as is in the following salad.

SUNNY DAY
POTATO SALAD

6 solar baked potatoes, diced
1 solar hard boiled egg, diced
1 kosher pickle, diced

2 stalks celery, diced
1 c. grated carrot
3 tbs. minced onion
5 tbs. olive oil
1 c. fresh mushrooms, chopped

Saute mushrooms in olive oil and cool. Marinate with lemon juice and onion. When vegetables are diced, add marinated mushrooms and chill in refrigerator for an hour.

CORN on COB

Sink your teeth into the mouth watering fresh corn cooked by solar technology.

Soak corn on the cob in the husk for about 1 hr. in salt water.

Place the corn in an oven roaster bag.

Put in solar oven for 30 min. Serve.

MIDDLE EAST SALAD

Lentils teamed up with mint and feta cheese create an unforgettable salad.

1 1/2 c. lentils
2 1/2 c. water

Cook lentils in dark covered pot about 2 hrs. or until lentils are tender but retain shape. Place cooked lentils in salad bowl and toss in the following ingredients.

1/2 c. red bell pepper, diced
1/2 c. chopped carrot
1/4 c. chopped red onion
1 tbs. fresh mint
1 tbs. fresh minced parsley
1 clove garlic, minced

Stir in the vinaigrette.

3/4 c. olive oil
1 tbs. white wine vinegar
2 tsp. lemon peel, grated
1/2 tsp. sea salt
1/2 tsp. fresh black pepper

Add 1 cup of crumbled feta cheese. Cover and refrigerate.

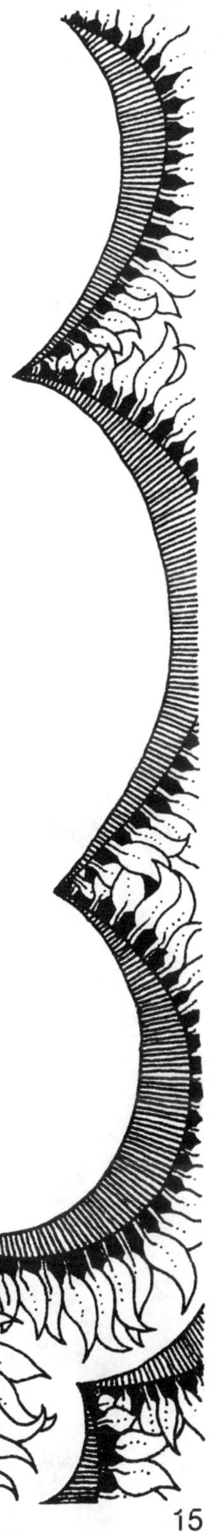

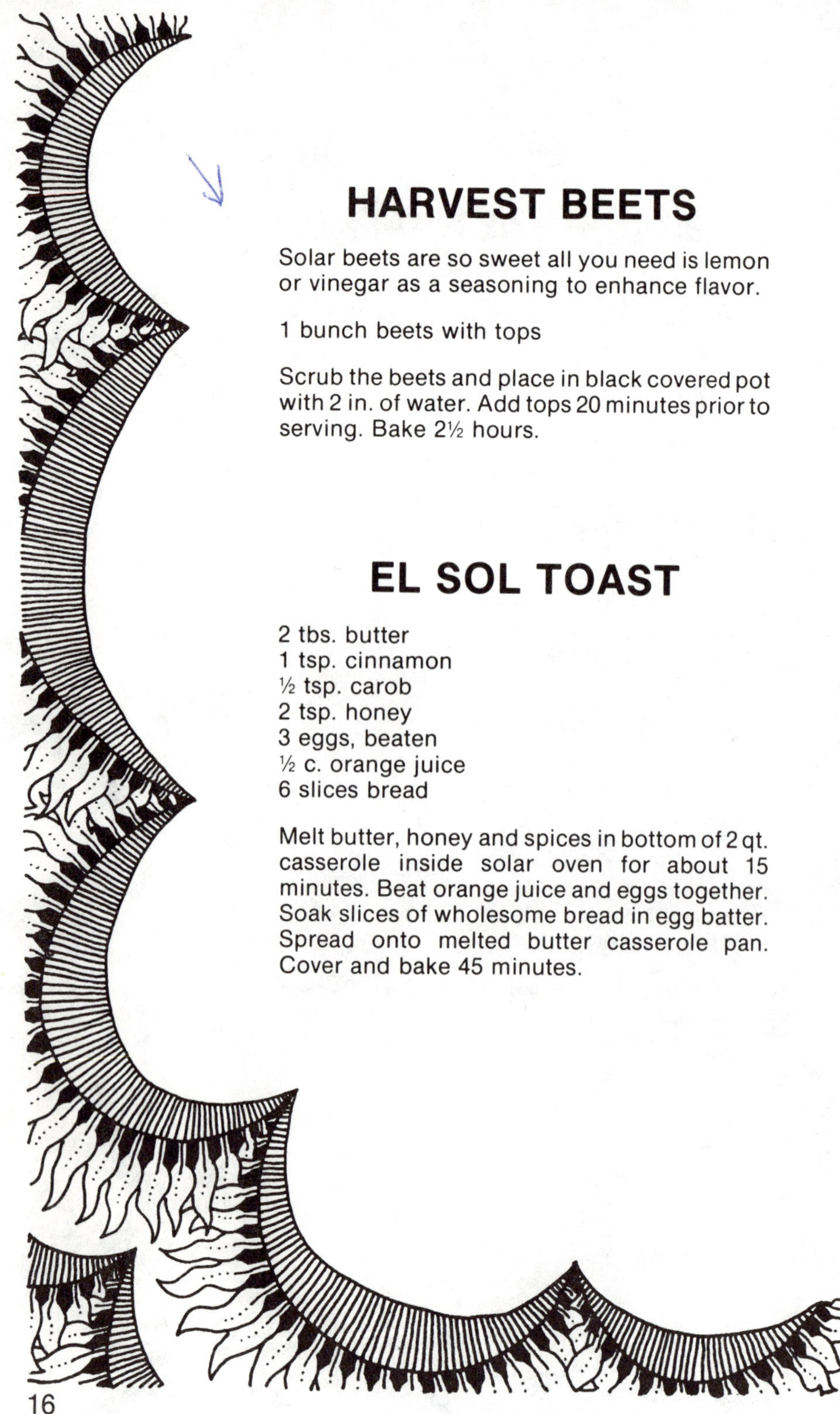

HARVEST BEETS

Solar beets are so sweet all you need is lemon or vinegar as a seasoning to enhance flavor.

1 bunch beets with tops

Scrub the beets and place in black covered pot with 2 in. of water. Add tops 20 minutes prior to serving. Bake 2½ hours.

EL SOL TOAST

2 tbs. butter
1 tsp. cinnamon
½ tsp. carob
2 tsp. honey
3 eggs, beaten
½ c. orange juice
6 slices bread

Melt butter, honey and spices in bottom of 2 qt. casserole inside solar oven for about 15 minutes. Beat orange juice and eggs together. Soak slices of wholesome bread in egg batter. Spread onto melted butter casserole pan. Cover and bake 45 minutes.

SUNRISE APRICOTS

Solarize fruit served over morning toast or in a hot cereal illuminates your break-fast.

1 c. dried apricots, chopped
1 c. water
1 tbs. honey
Pinch of cardamom and ground cloves
2 tbs. lemon juice

Soak apricots in water overnight. Next day, place in a small dark sauce pan with lid and simmer in solar oven 30 min. Stir in remaining ingredients and let cook for an additional 15 min.

*Almost any dried fruit can be prepared this way.

SAUCY APPLES

A hybrid between applesauce and baked apples. Mmmm.

8 apples, cut in slices with skins
2 tbs. orange juice concentrate
1/4 c. water

Core and cut apples. Place in dark roaster and drizzle liquid over them. Cover and bake 4 to 6 hours in solar oven.

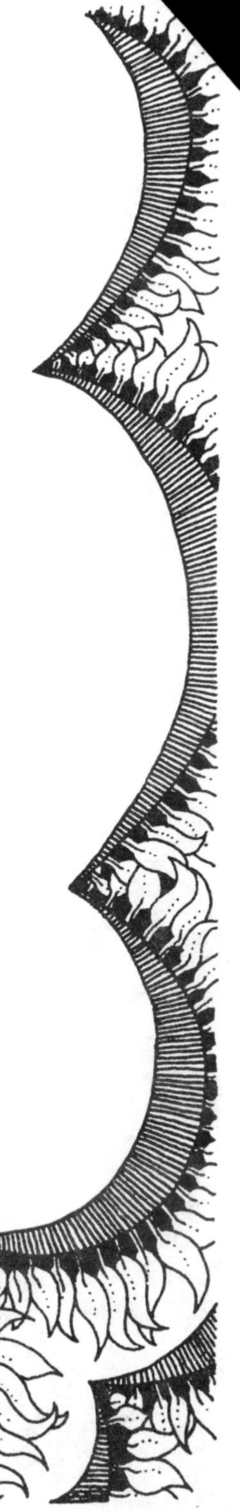

SOUPS

Soups can be created from leftovers or put together from a recipe. Whatever style they originate in, the beauty of each soup can never be exactly duplicated. Enjoy the process of soupmaking with a solar oven. Vegetables can be sauteed or uncooked and added directly to pre-heated or unheated broth to be sun-simmered. The options depend on the amount of sunlight available and how soon you want to serve the soup. The same soup can be ready by noon or appetizingly enjoyed for dinner.

ALL SEASON SOLAR SOUP

Endless variations are possible depending on whatever vegetables are in season.

5-6 c. water or vegetable stock
2 medium tomatoes,
3 celery stalks, diced
1 onion, diced
2 carrots, grated

3 broccoli stalks with flowers, sliced
Any leftover rice, millet or barley
1-2 tbs. peanut butter (*optional* - stock can be thickened with this)

Combine all ingredients in black pot with lid. Place in oven for 4 hrs. for flavors to be well mixed.

MISO SOUP

Miso is a fermented paste of soybeans, grains and salt. It is an all purpose base and a source of protein for soup stock. It can be obtained at oriental markets, co-ops and health outlets.

6 c. water	1 tsp. oil
1 onion, diced	2 tsp. honey
3 stalks celery, diced	Season with crushed
2 carrots, cut in	garlic
thin circles	1 tsp. freshly grated
1 c. shredded cabbage	ginger
1 c. mushrooms	2 tbs. miso
(optional)	

Place all ingredients in a black pot with lid. Before removing from oven mix two tablespoons of miso into soup. Simmer 15 minutes. Miso should not be boiled as this destroys its valuable digestive enzymes.

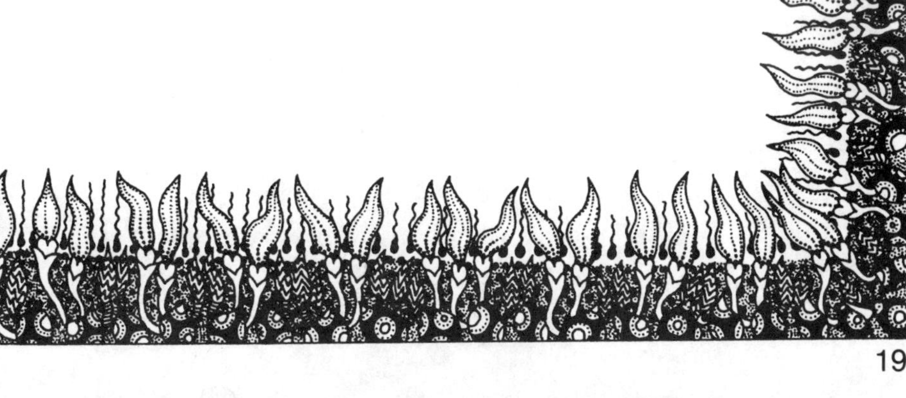

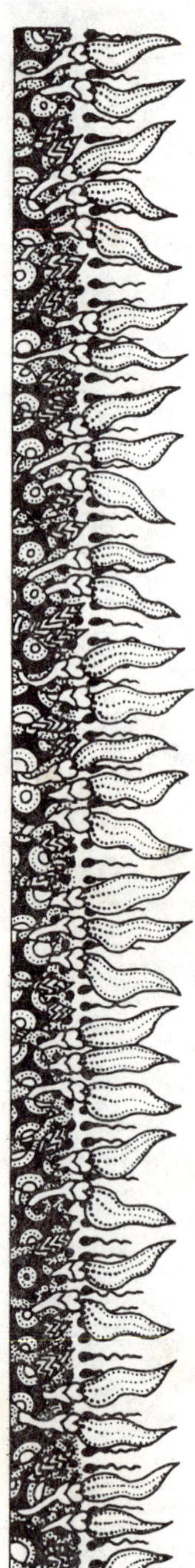

BOUNTIFUL BEAN SOUP

This soup can be made in quantities and frozen for a winter day to simmer in your solar oven.

1 c. mixed dried beans (navy, black, split peas,
   pinto, kidney)
Soak bean mixture overnight.

2 c. sliced smoked turkey sausage
1 large onion, chopped
3 cloves garlic, minced
1 tsp. chili powder
1 28 oz. can tomatoes, chopped
2 tbs. lemon juice

Place beans in large soup kettle, cover with a qt. of water and add turkey sausage. Cook about 3 hrs. Add the onion, garlic, chili powder, tomatoes and lemon juice. Cook another 2 hrs. Serve or freeze for winter use.

CHICKEN AND BARLEY

An old fashioned favorite.

1 whole chicken
1 c. barley

Place a whole chicken in a dark pot with water to cover. Cook with lid for 3 hours. In another pot, put one cup barley and two cups water. Cook same amount of time as chicken.

Add:
2 carrots, chopped
1 1/2 c. celery, diced
1 onion, diced
1 c. mushrooms, fresh
2 c. barley, cooked

Simmer in solar oven until supper. Peas are also a compatible ingredient.

SUMMER TOMATO SOUP

This soup derives its origin when too many vine-ripened tomatoes appear in a garden. It is a gourmet treat of Mother Nature.

1 dozen very ripe tomatoes	½ tsp. tamari/soy sauce
3 c. water (depends on consistency desired)	1 c. almonds
	½ c. carrot, grated
½ c. chopped parsley	½ c. celery, grated
1 onion, diced	¼ c. bell pepper, finely chopped

Skin and mash the tomatoes. Place in black pot with lid. Add vegetables. A half hour before serving, blend one cup almonds in 2 cups of water. Make into almond milk and mix into tomato soup.

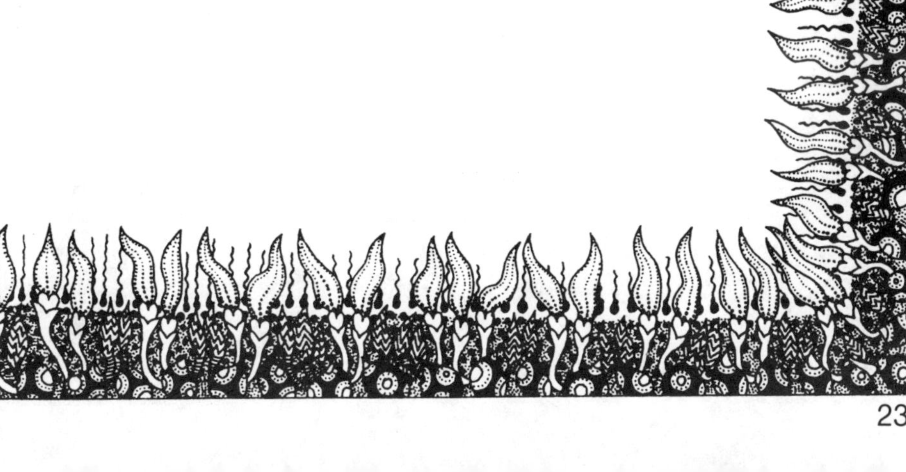

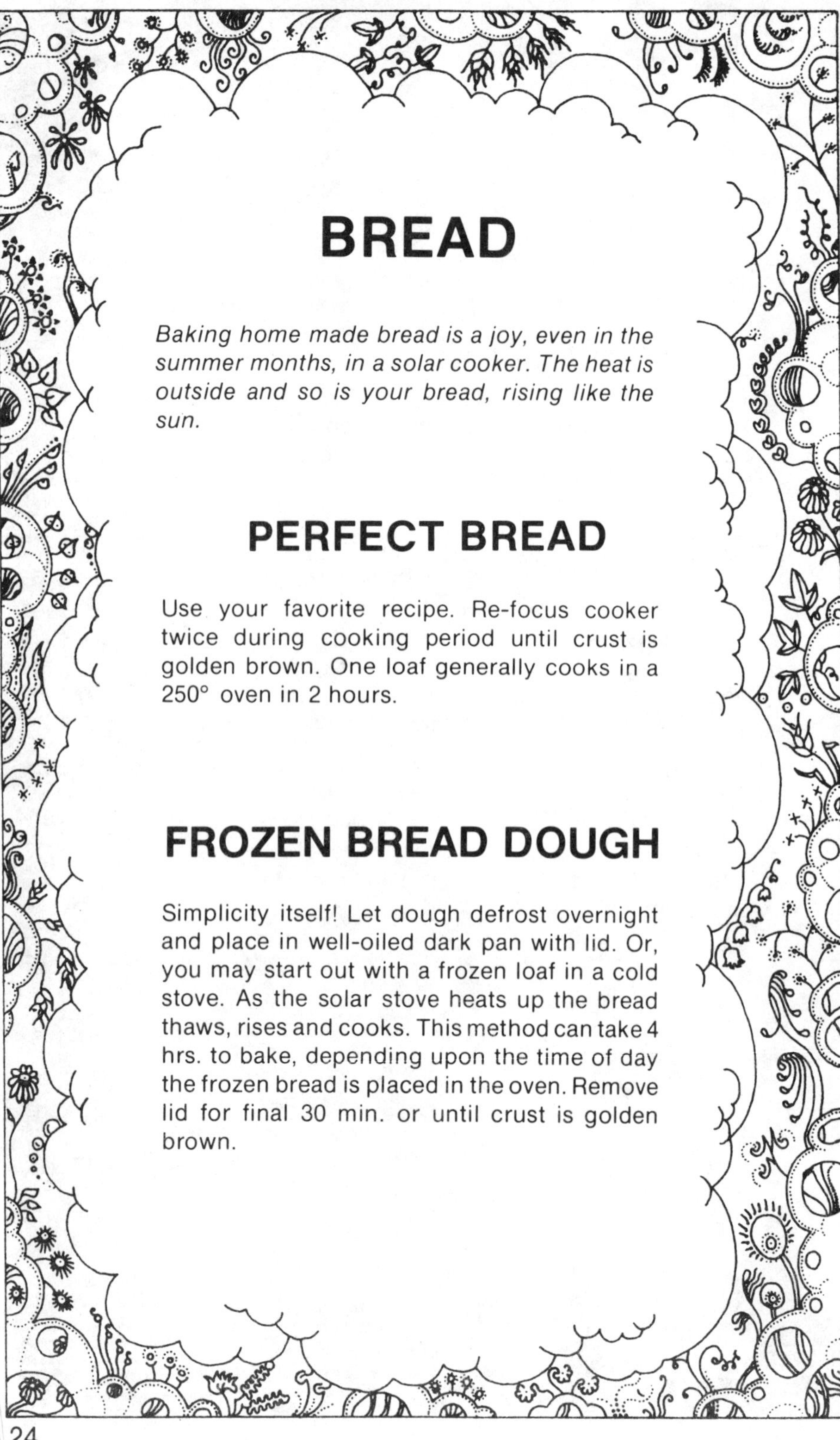

BREAD

Baking home made bread is a joy, even in the summer months, in a solar cooker. The heat is outside and so is your bread, rising like the sun.

PERFECT BREAD

Use your favorite recipe. Re-focus cooker twice during cooking period until crust is golden brown. One loaf generally cooks in a 250° oven in 2 hours.

FROZEN BREAD DOUGH

Simplicity itself! Let dough defrost overnight and place in well-oiled dark pan with lid. Or, you may start out with a frozen loaf in a cold stove. As the solar stove heats up the bread thaws, rises and cooks. This method can take 4 hrs. to bake, depending upon the time of day the frozen bread is placed in the oven. Remove lid for final 30 min. or until crust is golden brown.

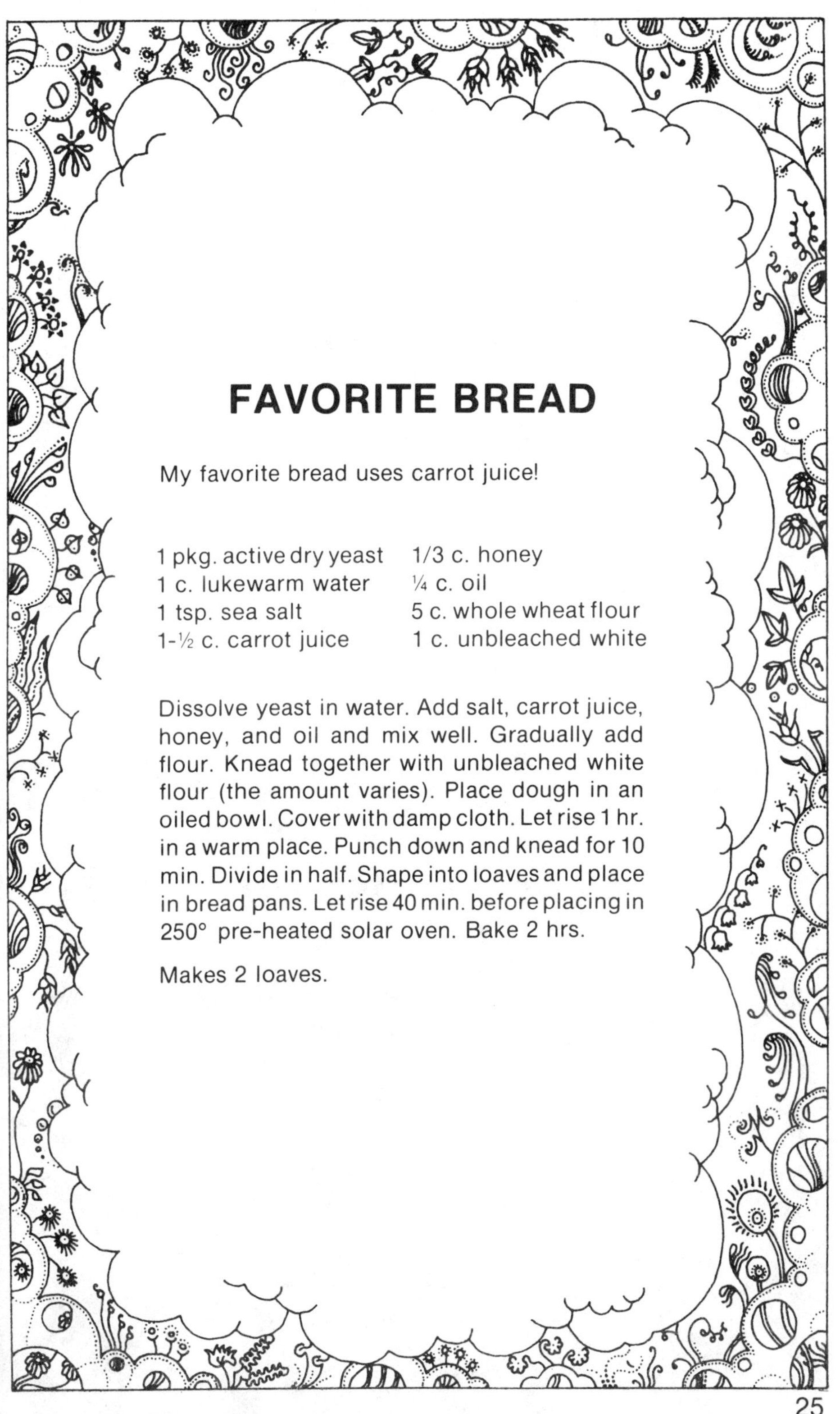

FAVORITE BREAD

My favorite bread uses carrot juice!

1 pkg. active dry yeast	1/3 c. honey
1 c. lukewarm water	¼ c. oil
1 tsp. sea salt	5 c. whole wheat flour
1-½ c. carrot juice	1 c. unbleached white

Dissolve yeast in water. Add salt, carrot juice, honey, and oil and mix well. Gradually add flour. Knead together with unbleached white flour (the amount varies). Place dough in an oiled bowl. Cover with damp cloth. Let rise 1 hr. in a warm place. Punch down and knead for 10 min. Divide in half. Shape into loaves and place in bread pans. Let rise 40 min. before placing in 250° pre-heated solar oven. Bake 2 hrs.

Makes 2 loaves.

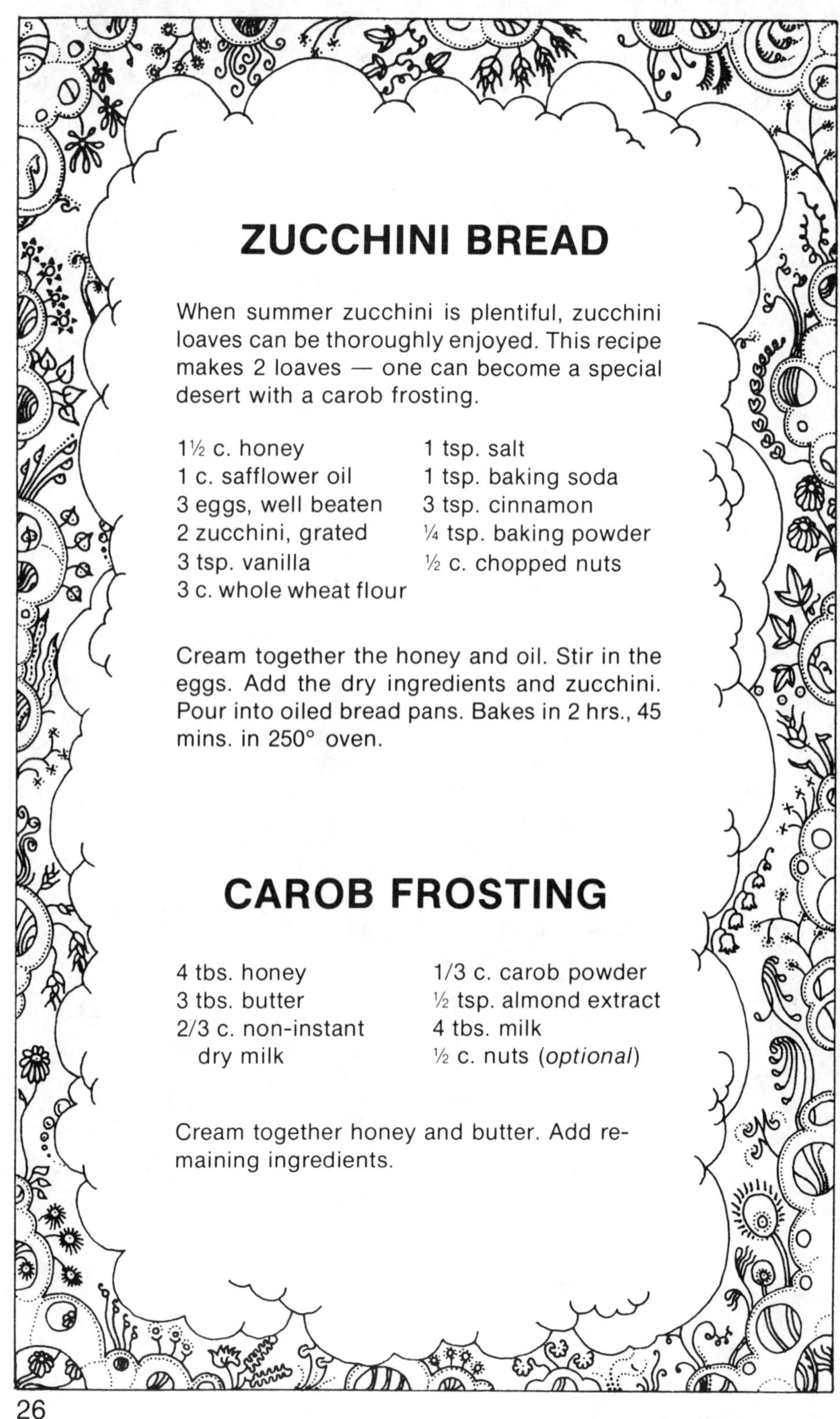

ZUCCHINI BREAD

When summer zucchini is plentiful, zucchini loaves can be thoroughly enjoyed. This recipe makes 2 loaves — one can become a special desert with a carob frosting.

1½ c. honey
1 c. safflower oil
3 eggs, well beaten
2 zucchini, grated
3 tsp. vanilla
3 c. whole wheat flour

1 tsp. salt
1 tsp. baking soda
3 tsp. cinnamon
¼ tsp. baking powder
½ c. chopped nuts

Cream together the honey and oil. Stir in the eggs. Add the dry ingredients and zucchini. Pour into oiled bread pans. Bakes in 2 hrs., 45 mins. in 250° oven.

CAROB FROSTING

4 tbs. honey
3 tbs. butter
2/3 c. non-instant
  dry milk

1/3 c. carob powder
½ tsp. almond extract
4 tbs. milk
½ c. nuts (*optional*)

Cream together honey and butter. Add remaining ingredients.

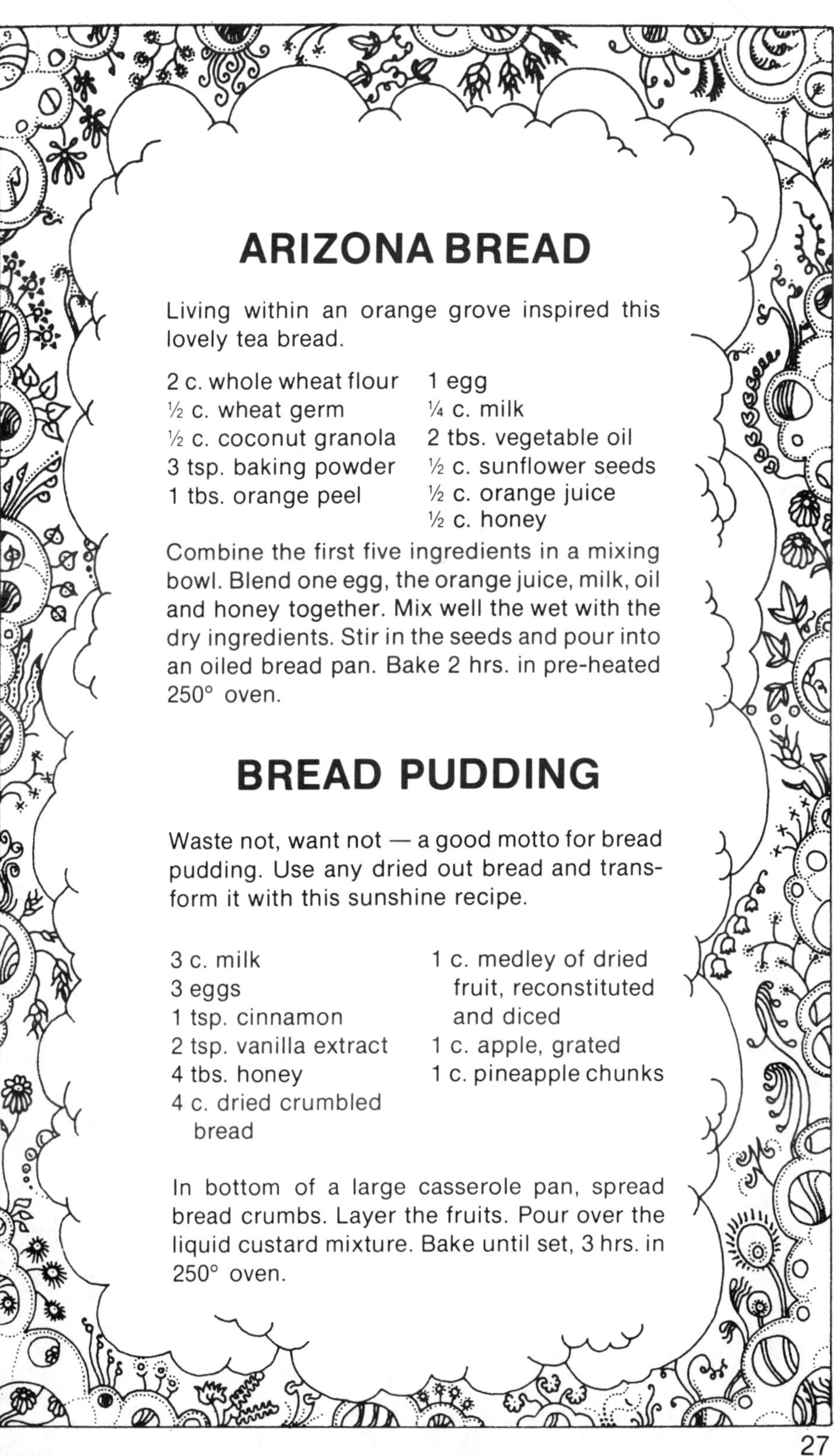

ARIZONA BREAD

Living within an orange grove inspired this lovely tea bread.

2 c. whole wheat flour
½ c. wheat germ
½ c. coconut granola
3 tsp. baking powder
1 tbs. orange peel

1 egg
¼ c. milk
2 tbs. vegetable oil
½ c. sunflower seeds
½ c. orange juice
½ c. honey

Combine the first five ingredients in a mixing bowl. Blend one egg, the orange juice, milk, oil and honey together. Mix well the wet with the dry ingredients. Stir in the seeds and pour into an oiled bread pan. Bake 2 hrs. in pre-heated 250° oven.

BREAD PUDDING

Waste not, want not — a good motto for bread pudding. Use any dried out bread and trans-form it with this sunshine recipe.

3 c. milk
3 eggs
1 tsp. cinnamon
2 tsp. vanilla extract
4 tbs. honey
4 c. dried crumbled
  bread

1 c. medley of dried
  fruit, reconstituted
  and diced
1 c. apple, grated
1 c. pineapple chunks

In bottom of a large casserole pan, spread bread crumbs. Layer the fruits. Pour over the liquid custard mixture. Bake until set, 3 hrs. in 250° oven.

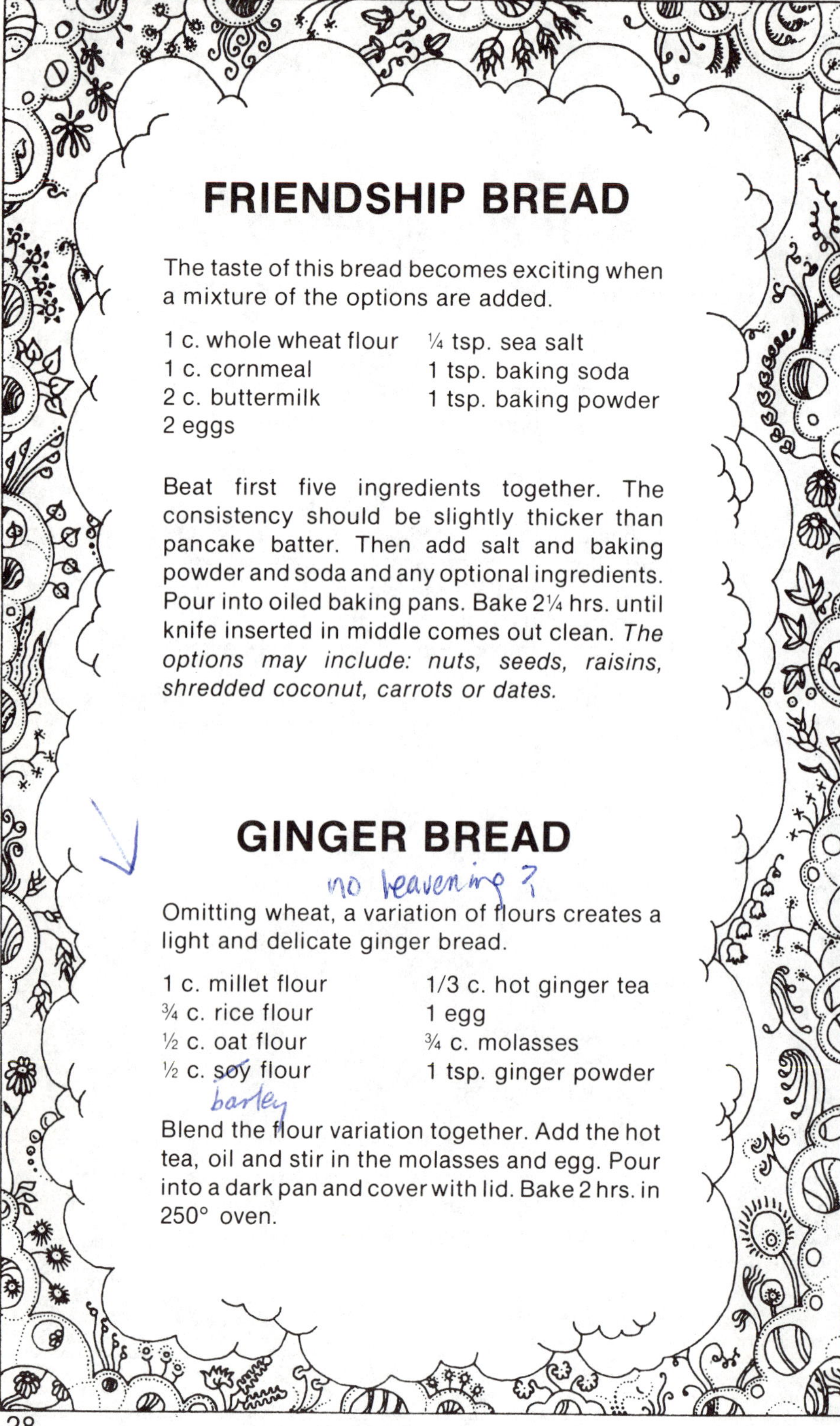

FRIENDSHIP BREAD

The taste of this bread becomes exciting when a mixture of the options are added.

1 c. whole wheat flour
1 c. cornmeal
2 c. buttermilk
2 eggs

¼ tsp. sea salt
1 tsp. baking soda
1 tsp. baking powder

Beat first five ingredients together. The consistency should be slightly thicker than pancake batter. Then add salt and baking powder and soda and any optional ingredients. Pour into oiled baking pans. Bake 2¼ hrs. until knife inserted in middle comes out clean. *The options may include: nuts, seeds, raisins, shredded coconut, carrots or dates.*

GINGER BREAD

Omitting wheat, a variation of flours creates a light and delicate ginger bread.

1 c. millet flour
¾ c. rice flour
½ c. oat flour
½ c. soy flour

1/3 c. hot ginger tea
1 egg
¾ c. molasses
1 tsp. ginger powder

Blend the flour variation together. Add the hot tea, oil and stir in the molasses and egg. Pour into a dark pan and cover with lid. Bake 2 hrs. in 250° oven.

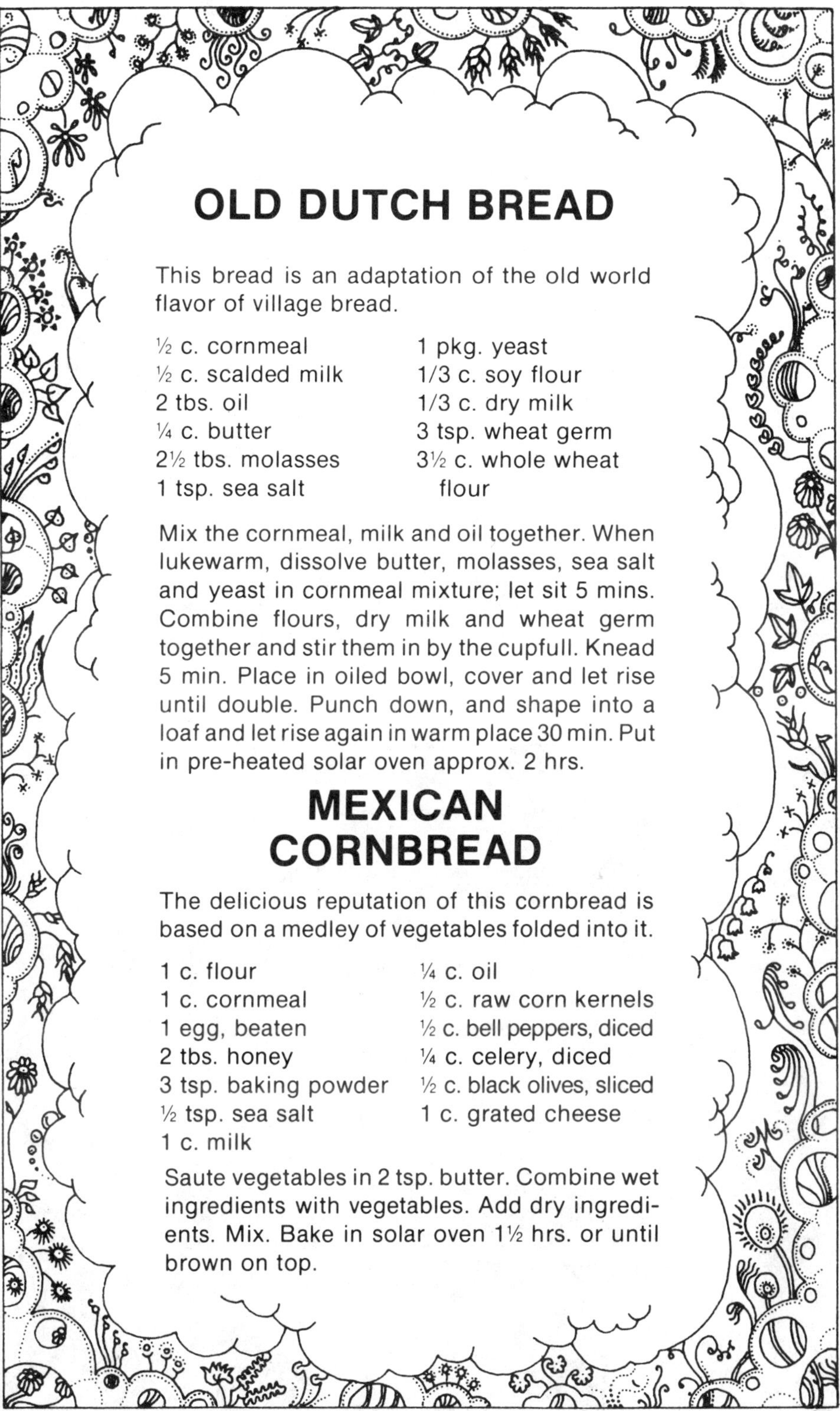

OLD DUTCH BREAD

This bread is an adaptation of the old world flavor of village bread.

½ c. cornmeal	1 pkg. yeast
½ c. scalded milk	1/3 c. soy flour
2 tbs. oil	1/3 c. dry milk
¼ c. butter	3 tsp. wheat germ
2½ tbs. molasses	3½ c. whole wheat
1 tsp. sea salt	flour

Mix the cornmeal, milk and oil together. When lukewarm, dissolve butter, molasses, sea salt and yeast in cornmeal mixture; let sit 5 mins. Combine flours, dry milk and wheat germ together and stir them in by the cupfull. Knead 5 min. Place in oiled bowl, cover and let rise until double. Punch down, and shape into a loaf and let rise again in warm place 30 min. Put in pre-heated solar oven approx. 2 hrs.

MEXICAN CORNBREAD

The delicious reputation of this cornbread is based on a medley of vegetables folded into it.

1 c. flour	¼ c. oil
1 c. cornmeal	½ c. raw corn kernels
1 egg, beaten	½ c. bell peppers, diced
2 tbs. honey	¼ c. celery, diced
3 tsp. baking powder	½ c. black olives, sliced
½ tsp. sea salt	1 c. grated cheese
1 c. milk	

Saute vegetables in 2 tsp. butter. Combine wet ingredients with vegetables. Add dry ingredients. Mix. Bake in solar oven 1½ hrs. or until brown on top.

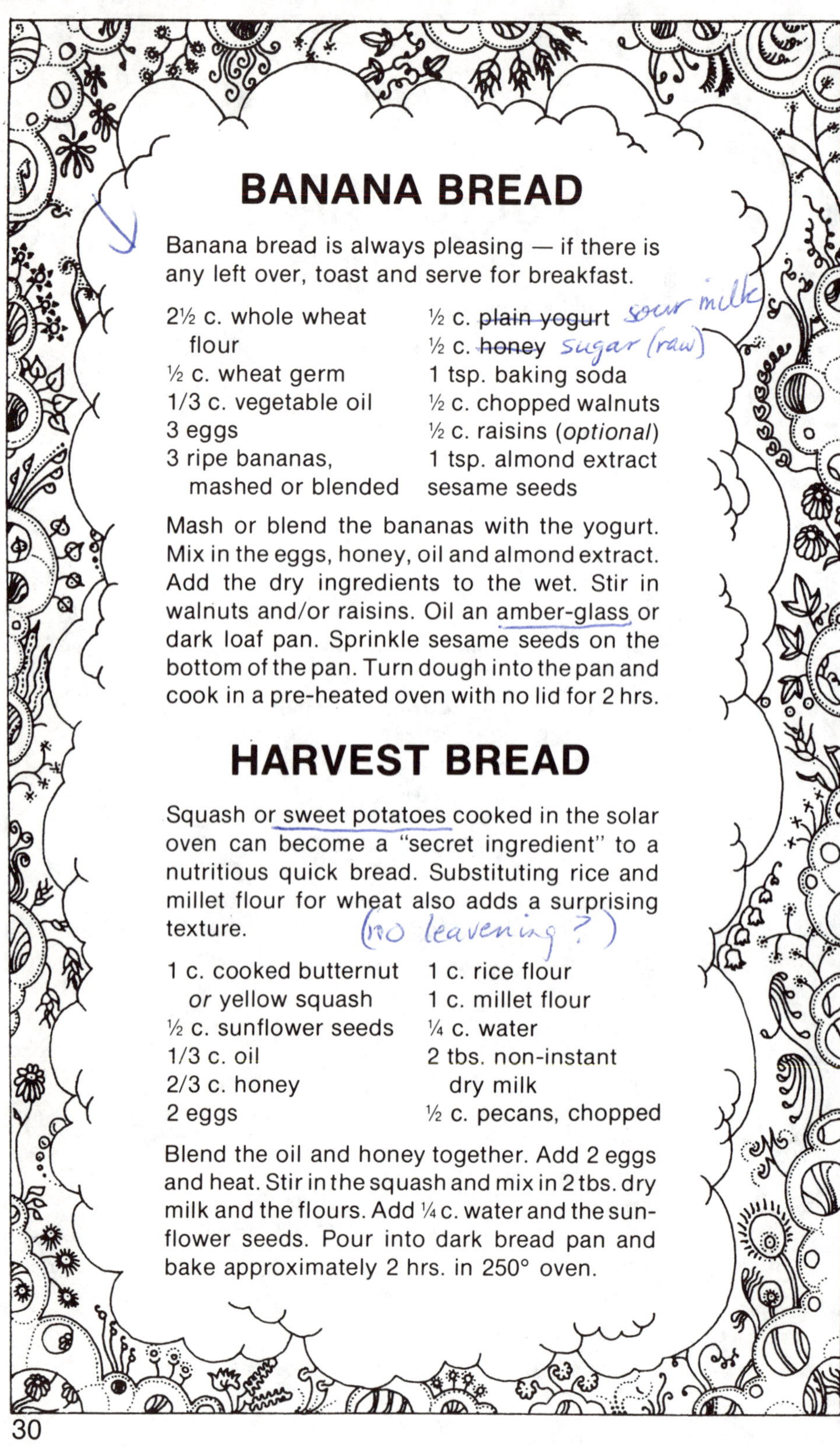

BANANA BREAD

Banana bread is always pleasing — if there is any left over, toast and serve for breakfast.

2½ c. whole wheat flour
½ c. wheat germ
1/3 c. vegetable oil
3 eggs
3 ripe bananas, mashed or blended

½ c. plain yogurt
½ c. honey
1 tsp. baking soda
½ c. chopped walnuts
½ c. raisins (*optional*)
1 tsp. almond extract
sesame seeds

Mash or blend the bananas with the yogurt. Mix in the eggs, honey, oil and almond extract. Add the dry ingredients to the wet. Stir in walnuts and/or raisins. Oil an amber-glass or dark loaf pan. Sprinkle sesame seeds on the bottom of the pan. Turn dough into the pan and cook in a pre-heated oven with no lid for 2 hrs.

HARVEST BREAD

Squash or sweet potatoes cooked in the solar oven can become a "secret ingredient" to a nutritious quick bread. Substituting rice and millet flour for wheat also adds a surprising texture.

1 c. cooked butternut *or* yellow squash
½ c. sunflower seeds
1/3 c. oil
2/3 c. honey
2 eggs

1 c. rice flour
1 c. millet flour
¼ c. water
2 tbs. non-instant dry milk
½ c. pecans, chopped

Blend the oil and honey together. Add 2 eggs and heat. Stir in the squash and mix in 2 tbs. dry milk and the flours. Add ¼ c. water and the sunflower seeds. Pour into dark bread pan and bake approximately 2 hrs. in 250° oven.

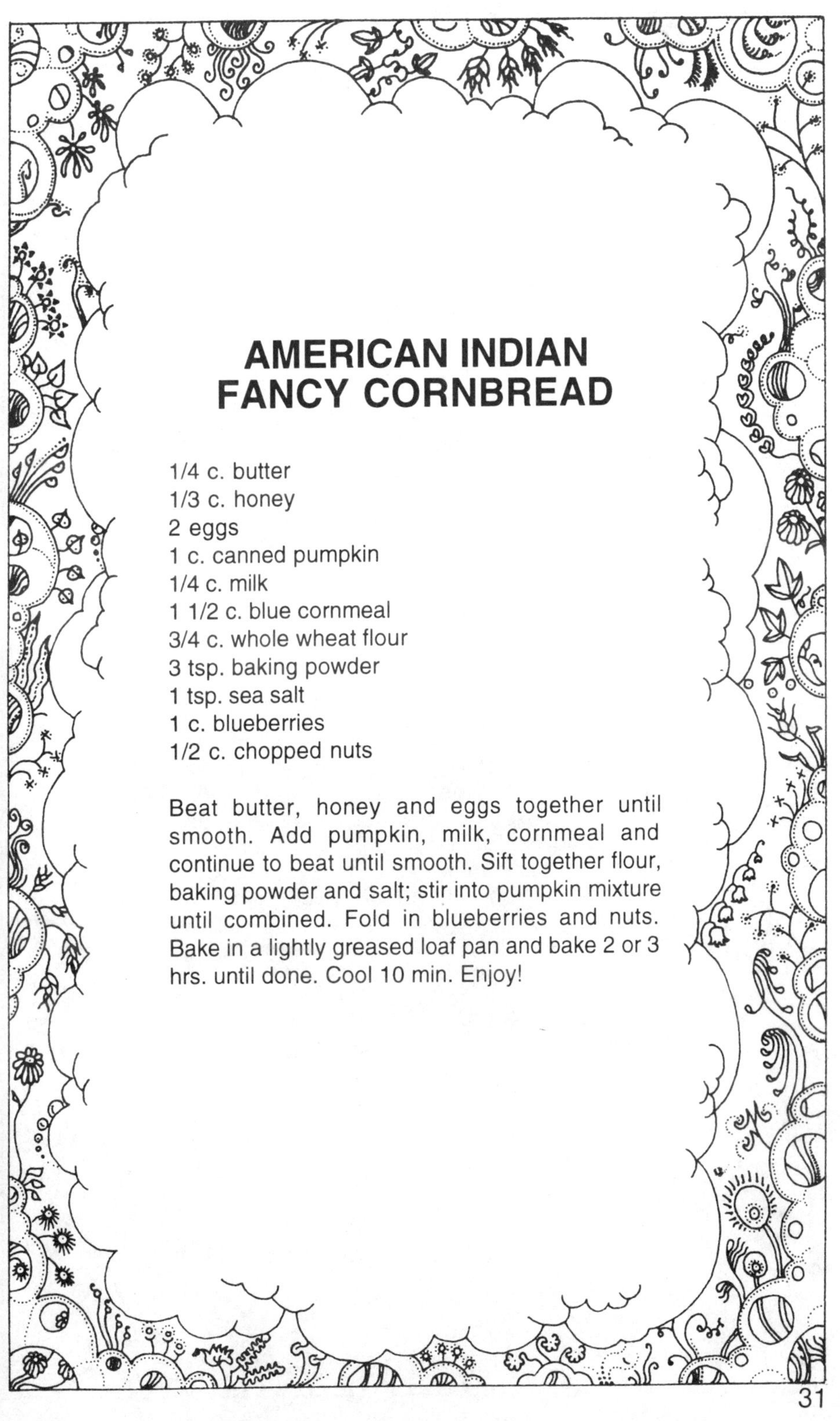

AMERICAN INDIAN FANCY CORNBREAD

1/4 c. butter
1/3 c. honey
2 eggs
1 c. canned pumpkin
1/4 c. milk
1 1/2 c. blue cornmeal
3/4 c. whole wheat flour
3 tsp. baking powder
1 tsp. sea salt
1 c. blueberries
1/2 c. chopped nuts

Beat butter, honey and eggs together until smooth. Add pumpkin, milk, cornmeal and continue to beat until smooth. Sift together flour, baking powder and salt; stir into pumpkin mixture until combined. Fold in blueberries and nuts. Bake in a lightly greased loaf pan and bake 2 or 3 hrs. until done. Cool 10 min. Enjoy!

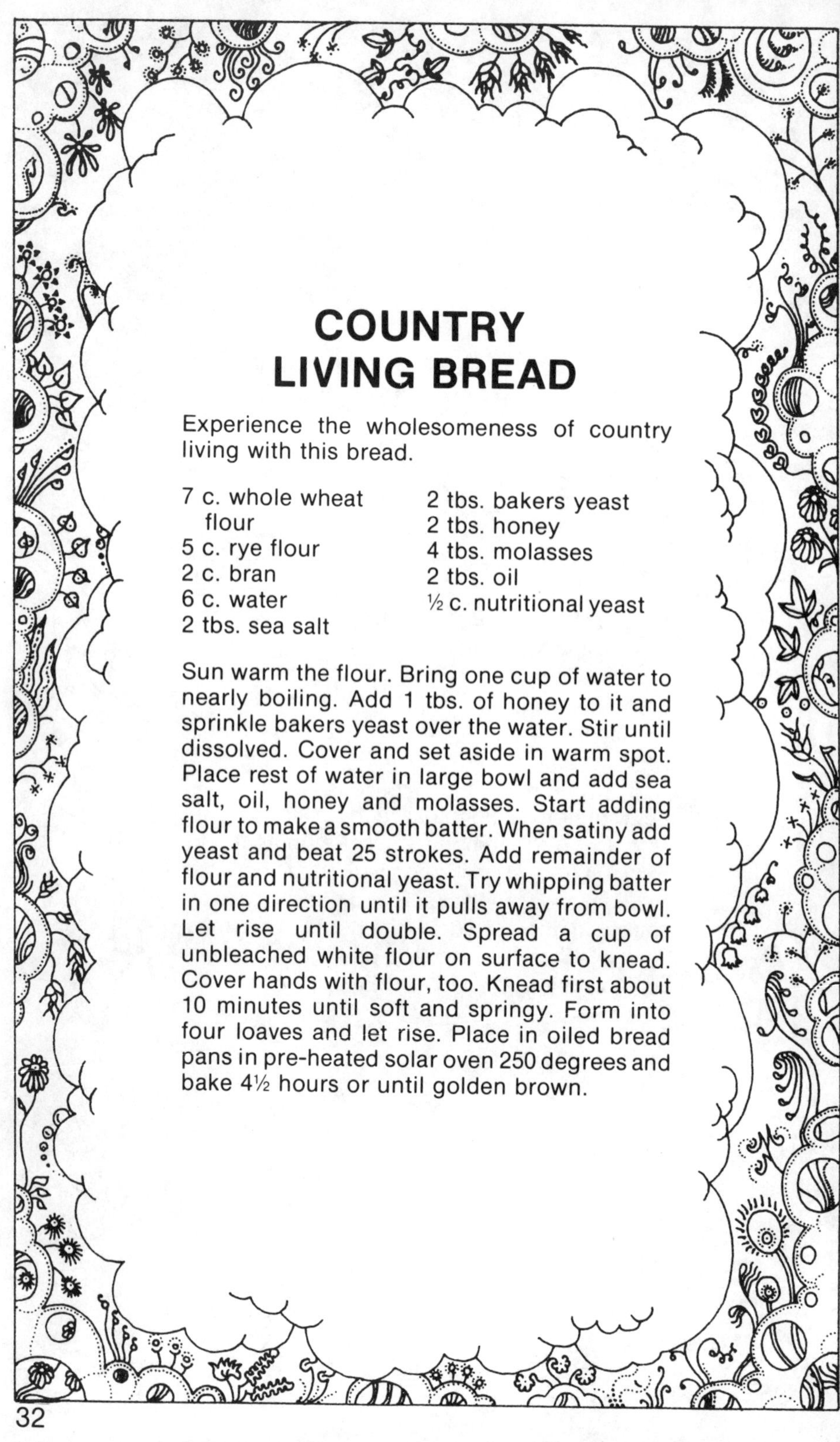

COUNTRY LIVING BREAD

Experience the wholesomeness of country living with this bread.

7 c. whole wheat flour
5 c. rye flour
2 c. bran
6 c. water
2 tbs. sea salt

2 tbs. bakers yeast
2 tbs. honey
4 tbs. molasses
2 tbs. oil
½ c. nutritional yeast

Sun warm the flour. Bring one cup of water to nearly boiling. Add 1 tbs. of honey to it and sprinkle bakers yeast over the water. Stir until dissolved. Cover and set aside in warm spot. Place rest of water in large bowl and add sea salt, oil, honey and molasses. Start adding flour to make a smooth batter. When satiny add yeast and beat 25 strokes. Add remainder of flour and nutritional yeast. Try whipping batter in one direction until it pulls away from bowl. Let rise until double. Spread a cup of unbleached white flour on surface to knead. Cover hands with flour, too. Knead first about 10 minutes until soft and springy. Form into four loaves and let rise. Place in oiled bread pans in pre-heated solar oven 250 degrees and bake 4½ hours or until golden brown.

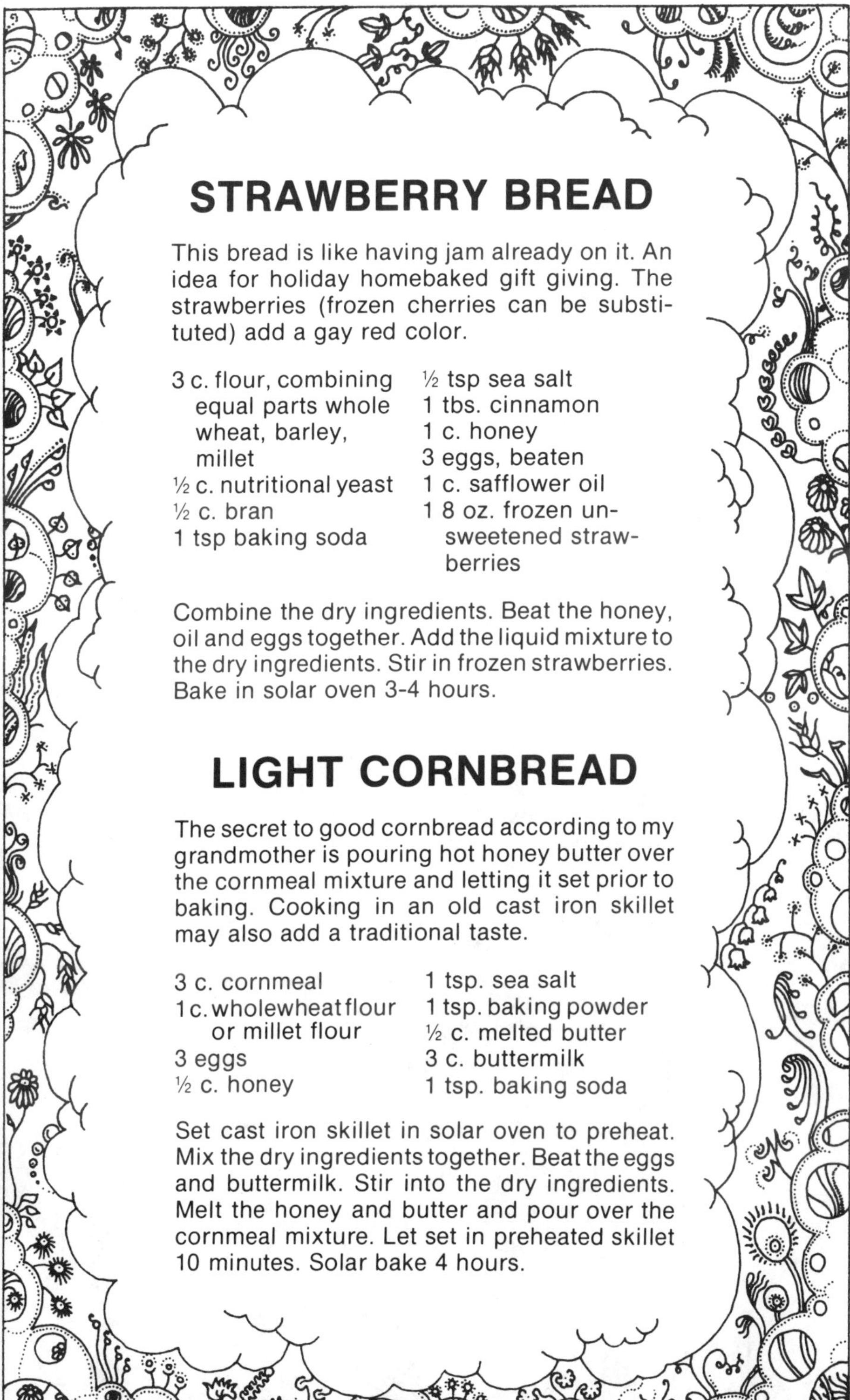

STRAWBERRY BREAD

This bread is like having jam already on it. An idea for holiday homebaked gift giving. The strawberries (frozen cherries can be substituted) add a gay red color.

3 c. flour, combining equal parts whole wheat, barley, millet
½ c. nutritional yeast
½ c. bran
1 tsp baking soda
½ tsp sea salt
1 tbs. cinnamon
1 c. honey
3 eggs, beaten
1 c. safflower oil
1 8 oz. frozen unsweetened strawberries

Combine the dry ingredients. Beat the honey, oil and eggs together. Add the liquid mixture to the dry ingredients. Stir in frozen strawberries. Bake in solar oven 3-4 hours.

LIGHT CORNBREAD

The secret to good cornbread according to my grandmother is pouring hot honey butter over the cornmeal mixture and letting it set prior to baking. Cooking in an old cast iron skillet may also add a traditional taste.

3 c. cornmeal
1 c. wholewheat flour or millet flour
3 eggs
½ c. honey
1 tsp. sea salt
1 tsp. baking powder
½ c. melted butter
3 c. buttermilk
1 tsp. baking soda

Set cast iron skillet in solar oven to preheat. Mix the dry ingredients together. Beat the eggs and buttermilk. Stir into the dry ingredients. Melt the honey and butter and pour over the cornmeal mixture. Let set in preheated skillet 10 minutes. Solar bake 4 hours.

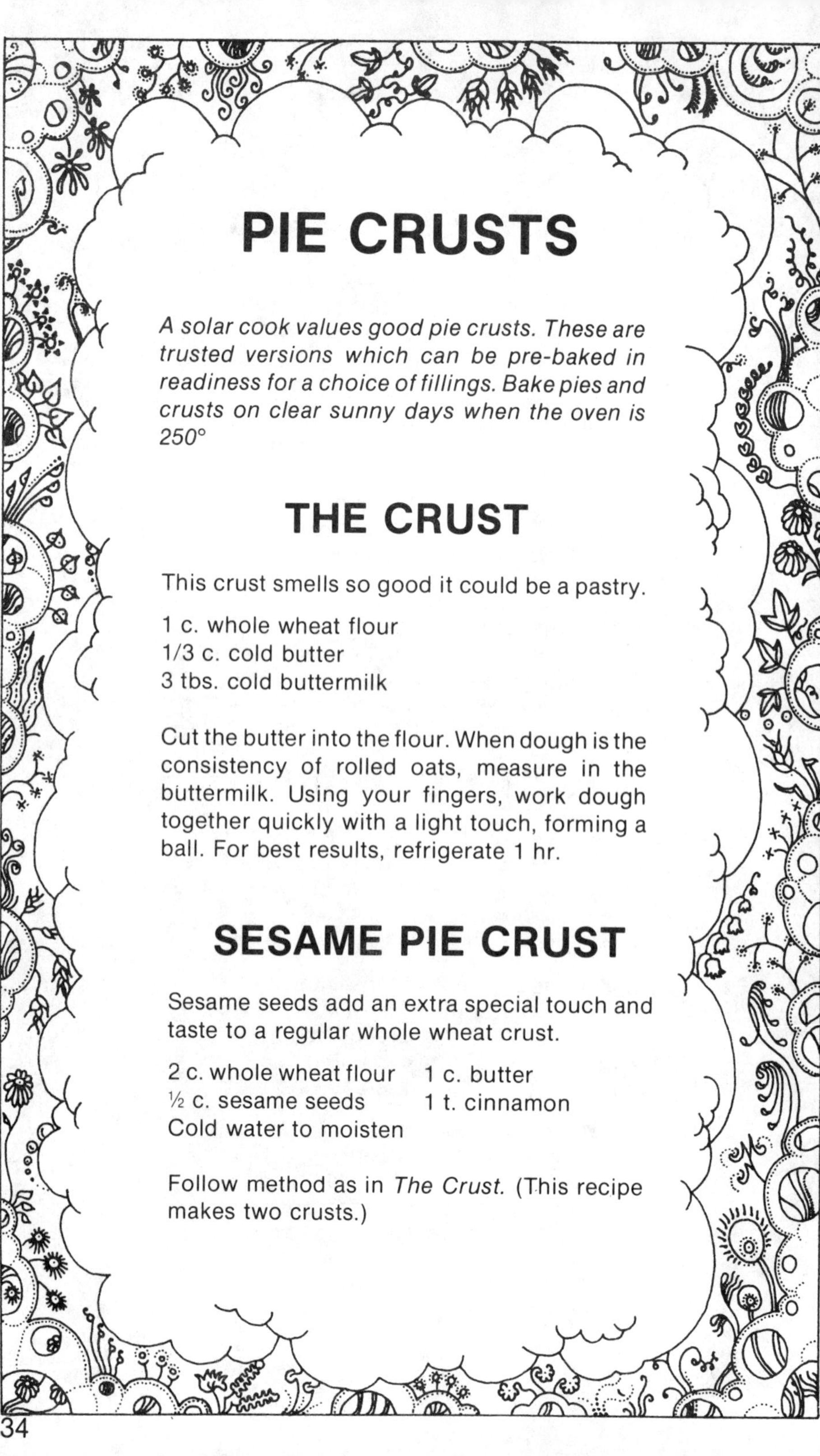

PIE CRUSTS

A solar cook values good pie crusts. These are trusted versions which can be pre-baked in readiness for a choice of fillings. Bake pies and crusts on clear sunny days when the oven is 250°

THE CRUST

This crust smells so good it could be a pastry.

1 c. whole wheat flour
1/3 c. cold butter
3 tbs. cold buttermilk

Cut the butter into the flour. When dough is the consistency of rolled oats, measure in the buttermilk. Using your fingers, work dough together quickly with a light touch, forming a ball. For best results, refrigerate 1 hr.

SESAME PIE CRUST

Sesame seeds add an extra special touch and taste to a regular whole wheat crust.

2 c. whole wheat flour   1 c. butter
½ c. sesame seeds   1 t. cinnamon
Cold water to moisten

Follow method as in *The Crust.* (This recipe makes two crusts.)

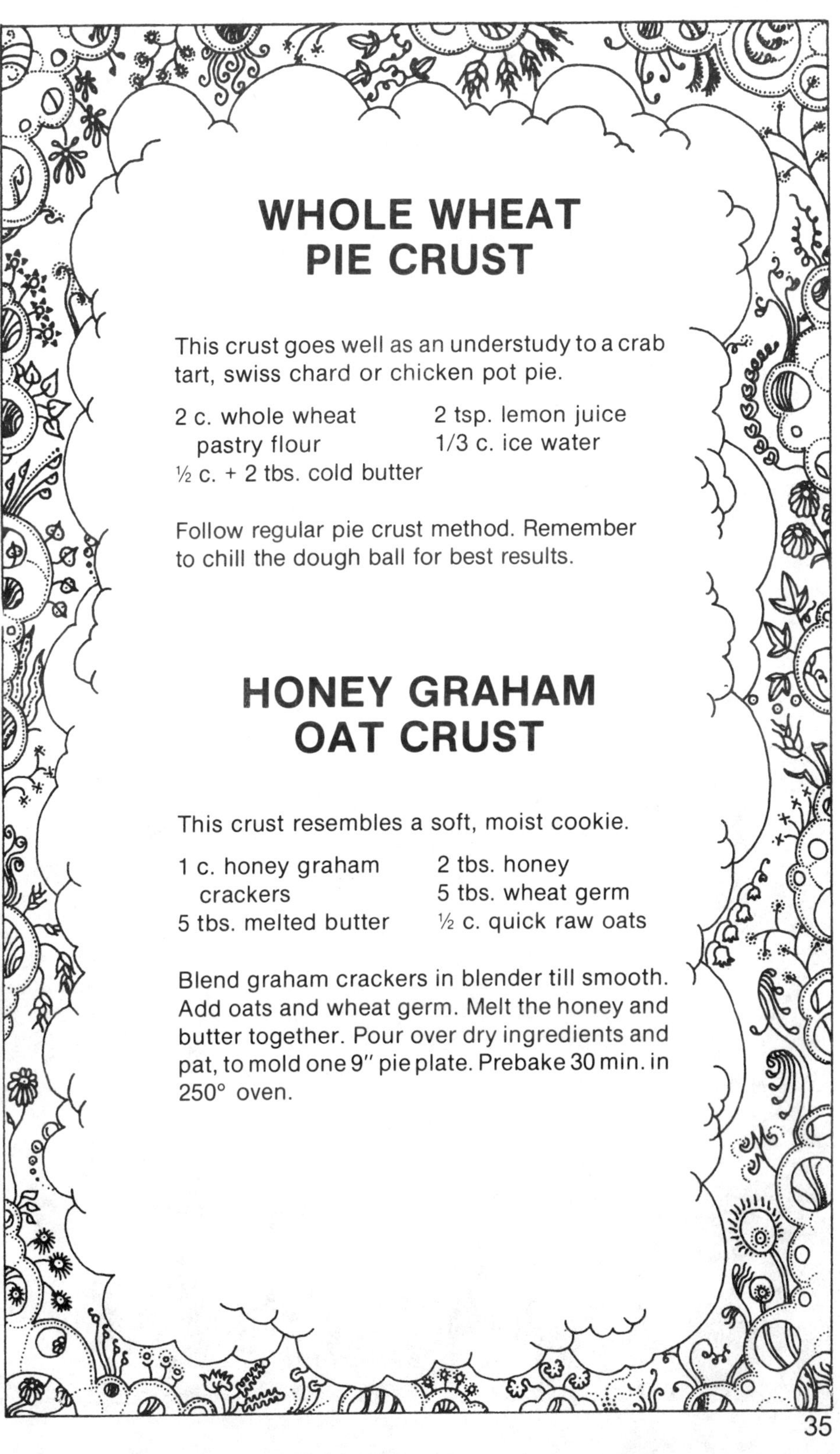

WHOLE WHEAT
PIE CRUST

This crust goes well as an understudy to a crab tart, swiss chard or chicken pot pie.

2 c. whole wheat
   pastry flour
½ c. + 2 tbs. cold butter

2 tsp. lemon juice
1/3 c. ice water

Follow regular pie crust method. Remember to chill the dough ball for best results.

HONEY GRAHAM
OAT CRUST

This crust resembles a soft, moist cookie.

1 c. honey graham
   crackers
5 tbs. melted butter

2 tbs. honey
5 tbs. wheat germ
½ c. quick raw oats

Blend graham crackers in blender till smooth. Add oats and wheat germ. Melt the honey and butter together. Pour over dry ingredients and pat, to mold one 9″ pie plate. Prebake 30 min. in 250° oven.

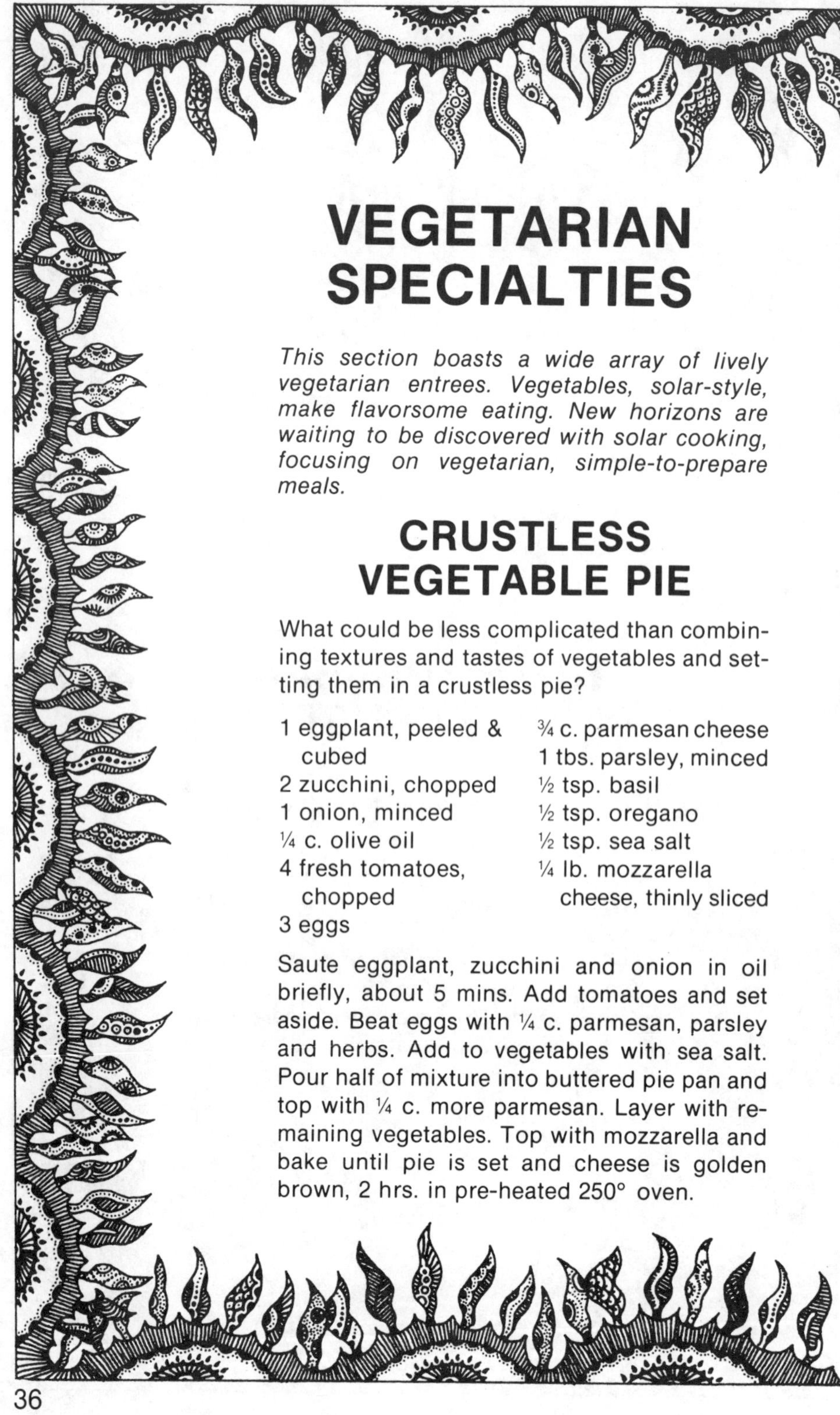

VEGETARIAN SPECIALTIES

This section boasts a wide array of lively vegetarian entrees. Vegetables, solar-style, make flavorsome eating. New horizons are waiting to be discovered with solar cooking, focusing on vegetarian, simple-to-prepare meals.

CRUSTLESS VEGETABLE PIE

What could be less complicated than combining textures and tastes of vegetables and setting them in a crustless pie?

1 eggplant, peeled & cubed
2 zucchini, chopped
1 onion, minced
¼ c. olive oil
4 fresh tomatoes, chopped
3 eggs
¾ c. parmesan cheese
1 tbs. parsley, minced
½ tsp. basil
½ tsp. oregano
½ tsp. sea salt
¼ lb. mozzarella cheese, thinly sliced

Saute eggplant, zucchini and onion in oil briefly, about 5 mins. Add tomatoes and set aside. Beat eggs with ¼ c. parmesan, parsley and herbs. Add to vegetables with sea salt. Pour half of mixture into buttered pie pan and top with ¼ c. more parmesan. Layer with remaining vegetables. Top with mozzarella and bake until pie is set and cheese is golden brown, 2 hrs. in pre-heated 250° oven.

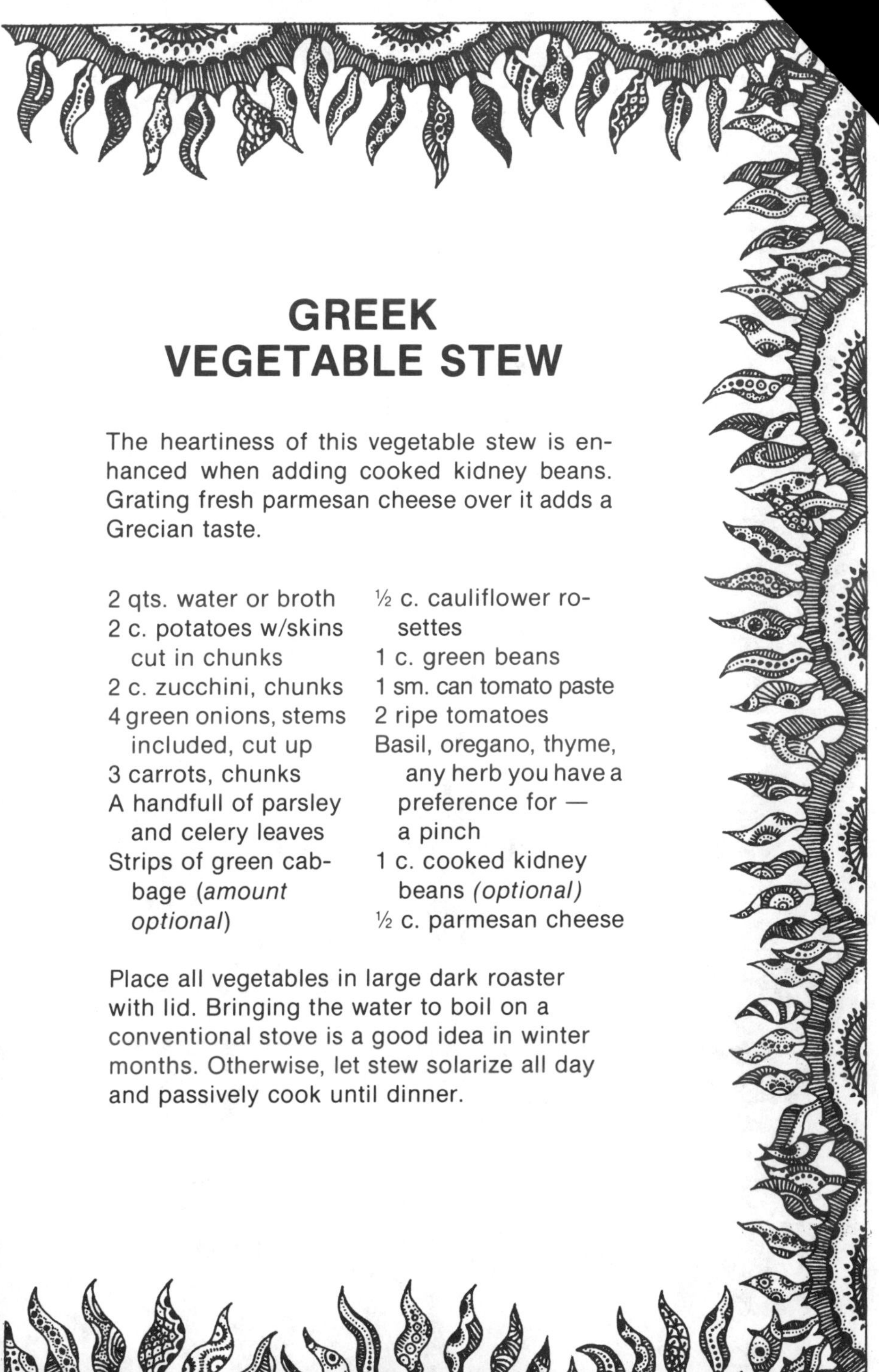

GREEK VEGETABLE STEW

The heartiness of this vegetable stew is enhanced when adding cooked kidney beans. Grating fresh parmesan cheese over it adds a Grecian taste.

2 qts. water or broth
2 c. potatoes w/skins cut in chunks
2 c. zucchini, chunks
4 green onions, stems included, cut up
3 carrots, chunks
A handfull of parsley and celery leaves
Strips of green cabbage (*amount optional*)

½ c. cauliflower rosettes
1 c. green beans
1 sm. can tomato paste
2 ripe tomatoes
Basil, oregano, thyme, any herb you have a preference for — a pinch
1 c. cooked kidney beans (*optional*)
½ c. parmesan cheese

Place all vegetables in large dark roaster with lid. Bringing the water to boil on a conventional stove is a good idea in winter months. Otherwise, let stew solarize all day and passively cook until dinner.

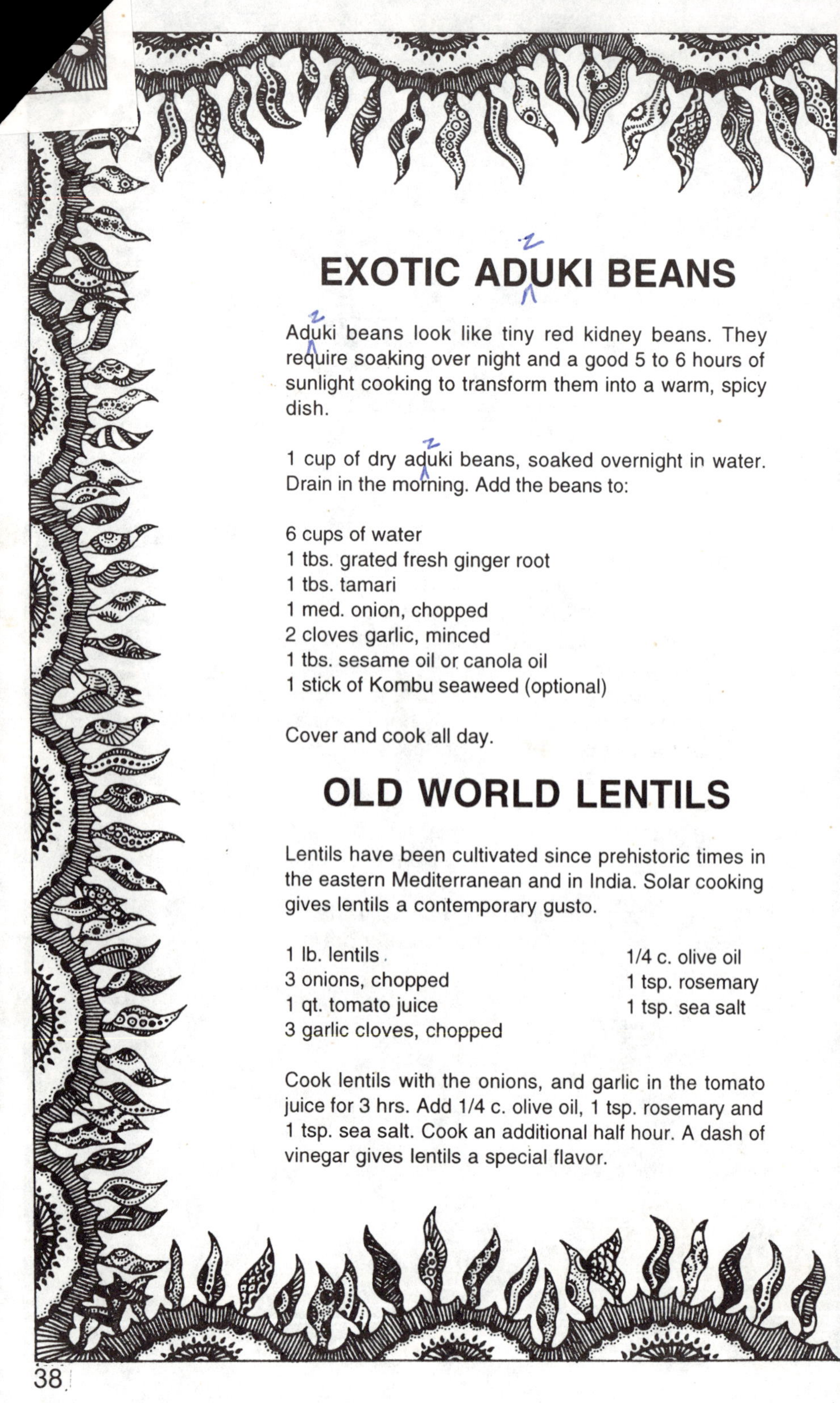

EXOTIC ADUKI BEANS

Aduki beans look like tiny red kidney beans. They require soaking over night and a good 5 to 6 hours of sunlight cooking to transform them into a warm, spicy dish.

1 cup of dry aduki beans, soaked overnight in water. Drain in the morning. Add the beans to:

6 cups of water
1 tbs. grated fresh ginger root
1 tbs. tamari
1 med. onion, chopped
2 cloves garlic, minced
1 tbs. sesame oil or canola oil
1 stick of Kombu seaweed (optional)

Cover and cook all day.

OLD WORLD LENTILS

Lentils have been cultivated since prehistoric times in the eastern Mediterranean and in India. Solar cooking gives lentils a contemporary gusto.

1 lb. lentils
3 onions, chopped
1 qt. tomato juice
3 garlic cloves, chopped

1/4 c. olive oil
1 tsp. rosemary
1 tsp. sea salt

Cook lentils with the onions, and garlic in the tomato juice for 3 hrs. Add 1/4 c. olive oil, 1 tsp. rosemary and 1 tsp. sea salt. Cook an additional half hour. A dash of vinegar gives lentils a special flavor.

RATATOUILLE

This combination of zucchini, tomato, and eggplant is a popular mediterranean stew..

1 medium eggplant, *peeled*, ½" cubes

3 small zucchini, *peeled*, 1" wedges

3 tomatoes, chunks

1 onion, sliced length-wise

3 cloves garlic, minced *¼ tsp. dried minced*

3 tsp. basil

½ tsp. oregano *(optional)*

1/3 c. olive oil *¼ c.*

1½ green pepper, cut ½ in. strips

½ c. tomato juice *→ or 1 can diced tomatoes*

Cut the vegetables accordingly. Add herbs. Place all ingredients in a dark casserole and sprinkle with olive oil and stir in tomato juice. Cover and bake 2 hrs. or until vegetables are *(4 hours 2–6 pm)* tender. Serve on bed of solar rice or cooked wheatberries, for pilaf.

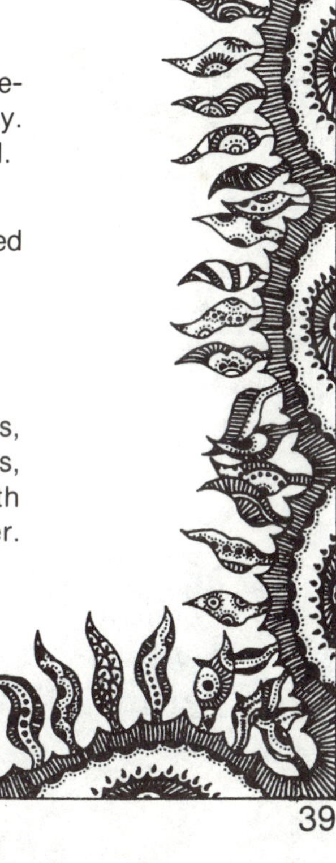

ITALIAN ZUCCHINI

The versatility of zucchini makes this vegetable popular. Italian zucchini is light and tasty. Serve with hot solar bread and sprout salad.

6 zucchini, cut in quarters

1 sm. spanish onion, thinly sliced

6 fresh tomatoes, thinly sliced

½ lb. mozzarella cheese, thinly sliced

2 tsp. basil

2 tsp. oregano

4 tbs. butter

¼ c. water

Butter a baking dish and layer the vegetables, beginning with the zucchini, onion, tomatoes, and mozzarella. Season with herbs, dot with butter. Add small amount of water and cover. Cook 2 hrs. or until zucchini is tender.

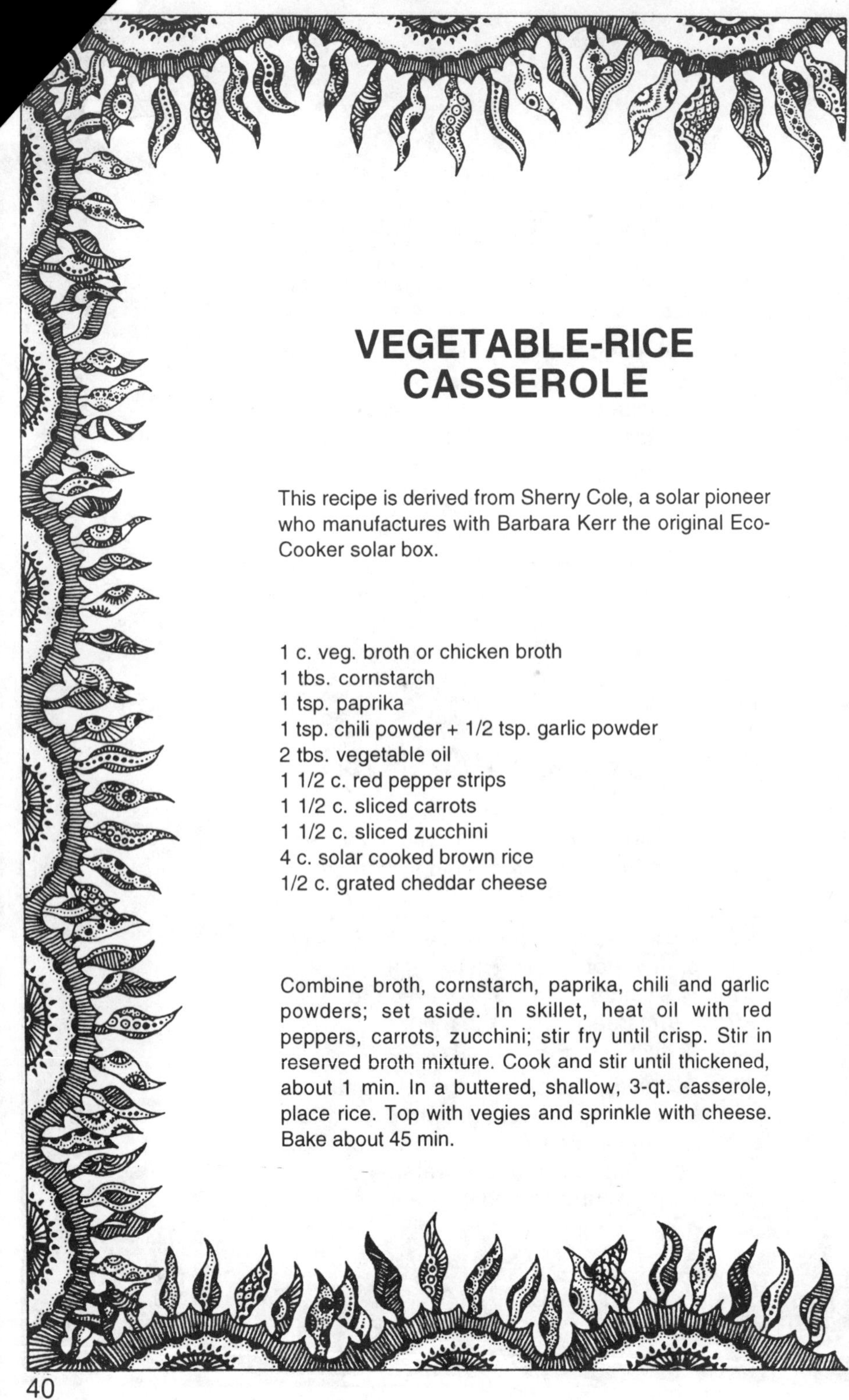

VEGETABLE-RICE CASSEROLE

This recipe is derived from Sherry Cole, a solar pioneer who manufactures with Barbara Kerr the original Eco-Cooker solar box.

1 c. veg. broth or chicken broth
1 tbs. cornstarch
1 tsp. paprika
1 tsp. chili powder + 1/2 tsp. garlic powder
2 tbs. vegetable oil
1 1/2 c. red pepper strips
1 1/2 c. sliced carrots
1 1/2 c. sliced zucchini
4 c. solar cooked brown rice
1/2 c. grated cheddar cheese

Combine broth, cornstarch, paprika, chili and garlic powders; set aside. In skillet, heat oil with red peppers, carrots, zucchini; stir fry until crisp. Stir in reserved broth mixture. Cook and stir until thickened, about 1 min. In a buttered, shallow, 3-qt. casserole, place rice. Top with vegies and sprinkle with cheese. Bake about 45 min.

MILLET LOAF

This loaf is an agreeable mixture of millet, vegetables and ground nuts. Full of healthy ingredients, it is a company pleaser.

2 c. cooked millet
1 bell pepper, chopped
1 onion, chopped
1 carrot, shredded
2 stalks celery, chopped
1 tsp. sea salt
4 tbs. lemon juice
½ c. ground sun-
flower seeds (try
walnuts or almonds
ground in blender)

3 tsp. tamari
2 c. wheat germ, bran
  or bread crumbs
1 c. monterey jack
  cheese, grated
1 c. non-instant dry
  milk
1 c. milk
2 eggs, slightly beaten
3 tbs. tahini
Season with basil

Mix and bake in oiled baking dish until golden brown. On overcast days, vegetables can be sauteed before mixing. Cook 1½ hrs. in 250° oven or 3-4 hrs. in 220° winter oven.

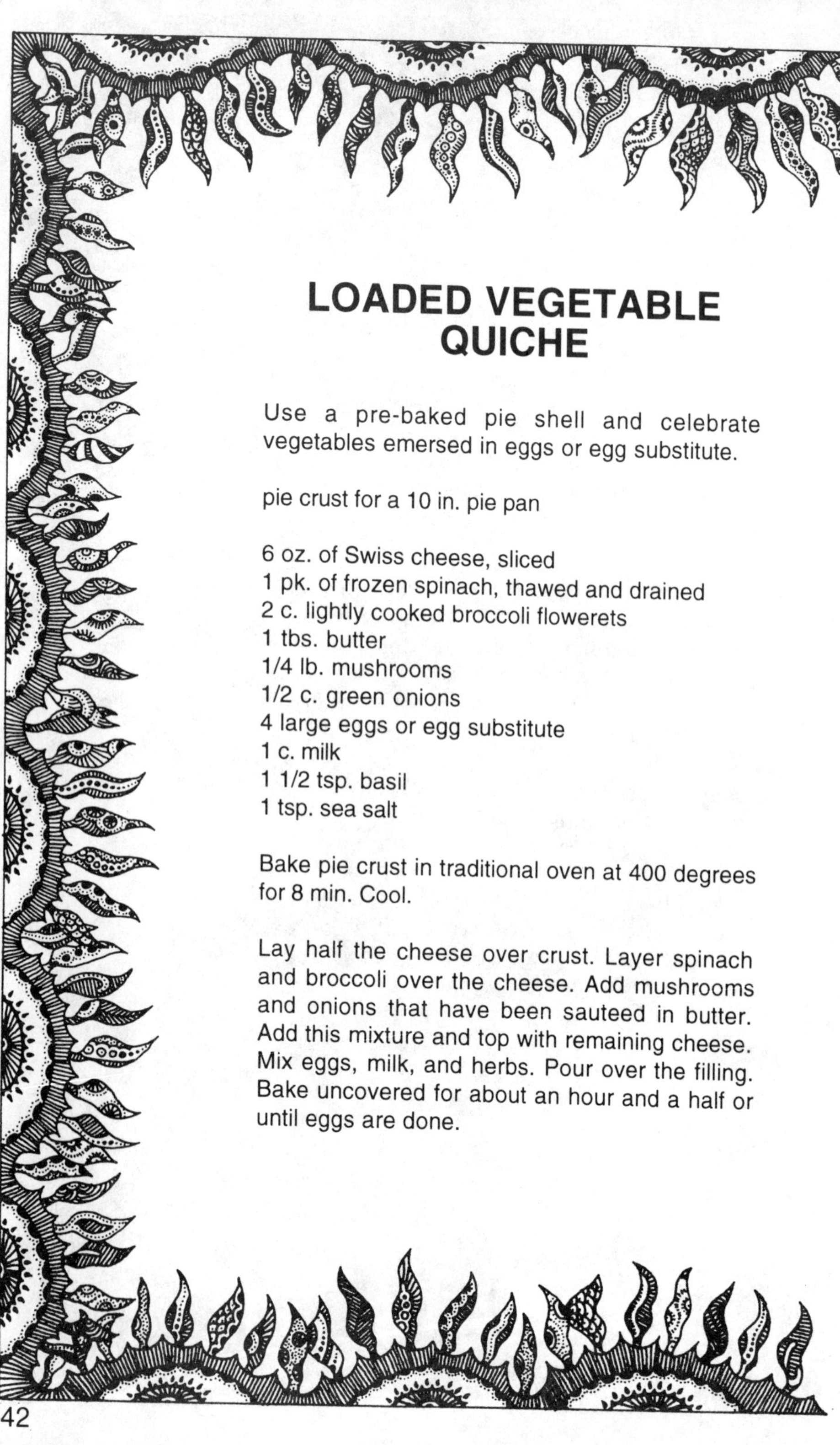

LOADED VEGETABLE QUICHE

Use a pre-baked pie shell and celebrate vegetables emersed in eggs or egg substitute.

pie crust for a 10 in. pie pan

6 oz. of Swiss cheese, sliced
1 pk. of frozen spinach, thawed and drained
2 c. lightly cooked broccoli flowerets
1 tbs. butter
1/4 lb. mushrooms
1/2 c. green onions
4 large eggs or egg substitute
1 c. milk
1 1/2 tsp. basil
1 tsp. sea salt

Bake pie crust in traditional oven at 400 degrees for 8 min. Cool.

Lay half the cheese over crust. Layer spinach and broccoli over the cheese. Add mushrooms and onions that have been sauteed in butter. Add this mixture and top with remaining cheese. Mix eggs, milk, and herbs. Pour over the filling. Bake uncovered for about an hour and a half or until eggs are done.

CHILI RELLENO

A souffle-like dish that cooks superbly, even on overcast days. Bake until a knife inserted comes out clean.

1 lb. whole green chilies	8 eggs, well beaten
2 c. grated cheddar cheese	½ tsp. cumin
	1½ c. milk
	3 tbs. whole wheat flour

Layer alternately the chili peppers and cheese in an oiled 9 x 13 dark casserole dish. Combine the beaten eggs, milk, flour and cumin powder. Pour this mixture over the peppers and cheese. Bake in 250° oven about 2 hrs. Watch carefully, eggs can overcook and become rubbery.

CHILI CORN CASSEROLE

This corn version with chilies and creamed corn is a substantial main course. Serve with sliced avocadoes and salsa for a Southwestern style dinner.

2 cans creamed corn	½ c. oil
1 c. yellow cornmeal	2 4-oz. cans diced green chilies
1½ c. milk	
2 eggs	1 c. grated cheese, jack or cheddar
1 tsp. baking powder	

Combine all ingredients. Pour into 9 x 13 baking dish. Bake covered in preheated oven 3-4 hrs., depending on season of year.

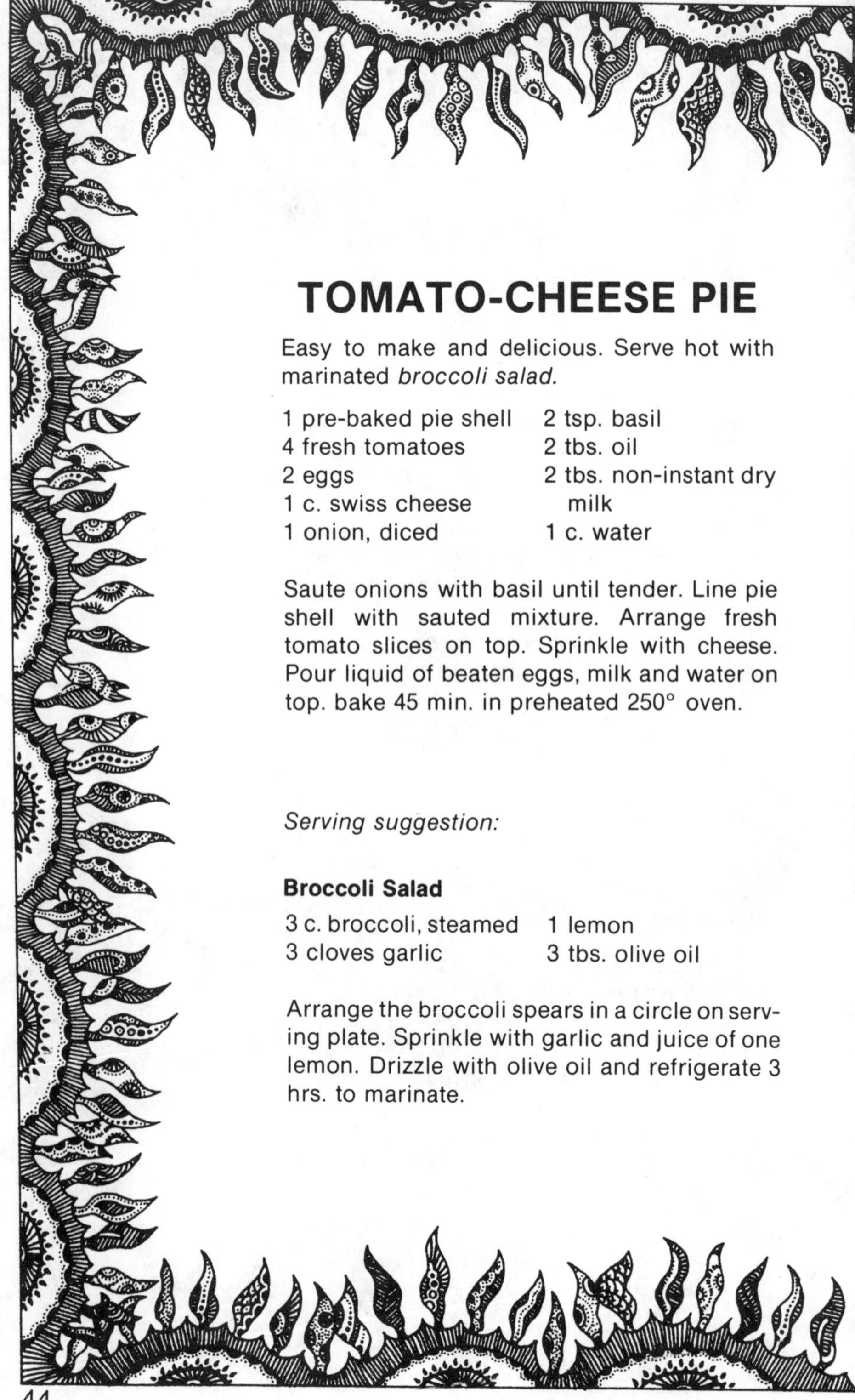

TOMATO-CHEESE PIE

Easy to make and delicious. Serve hot with marinated *broccoli salad*.

1 pre-baked pie shell	2 tsp. basil
4 fresh tomatoes	2 tbs. oil
2 eggs	2 tbs. non-instant dry
1 c. swiss cheese	milk
1 onion, diced	1 c. water

Saute onions with basil until tender. Line pie shell with sauted mixture. Arrange fresh tomato slices on top. Sprinkle with cheese. Pour liquid of beaten eggs, milk and water on top. bake 45 min. in preheated 250° oven.

Serving suggestion:

Broccoli Salad

3 c. broccoli, steamed	1 lemon
3 cloves garlic	3 tbs. olive oil

Arrange the broccoli spears in a circle on serving plate. Sprinkle with garlic and juice of one lemon. Drizzle with olive oil and refrigerate 3 hrs. to marinate.

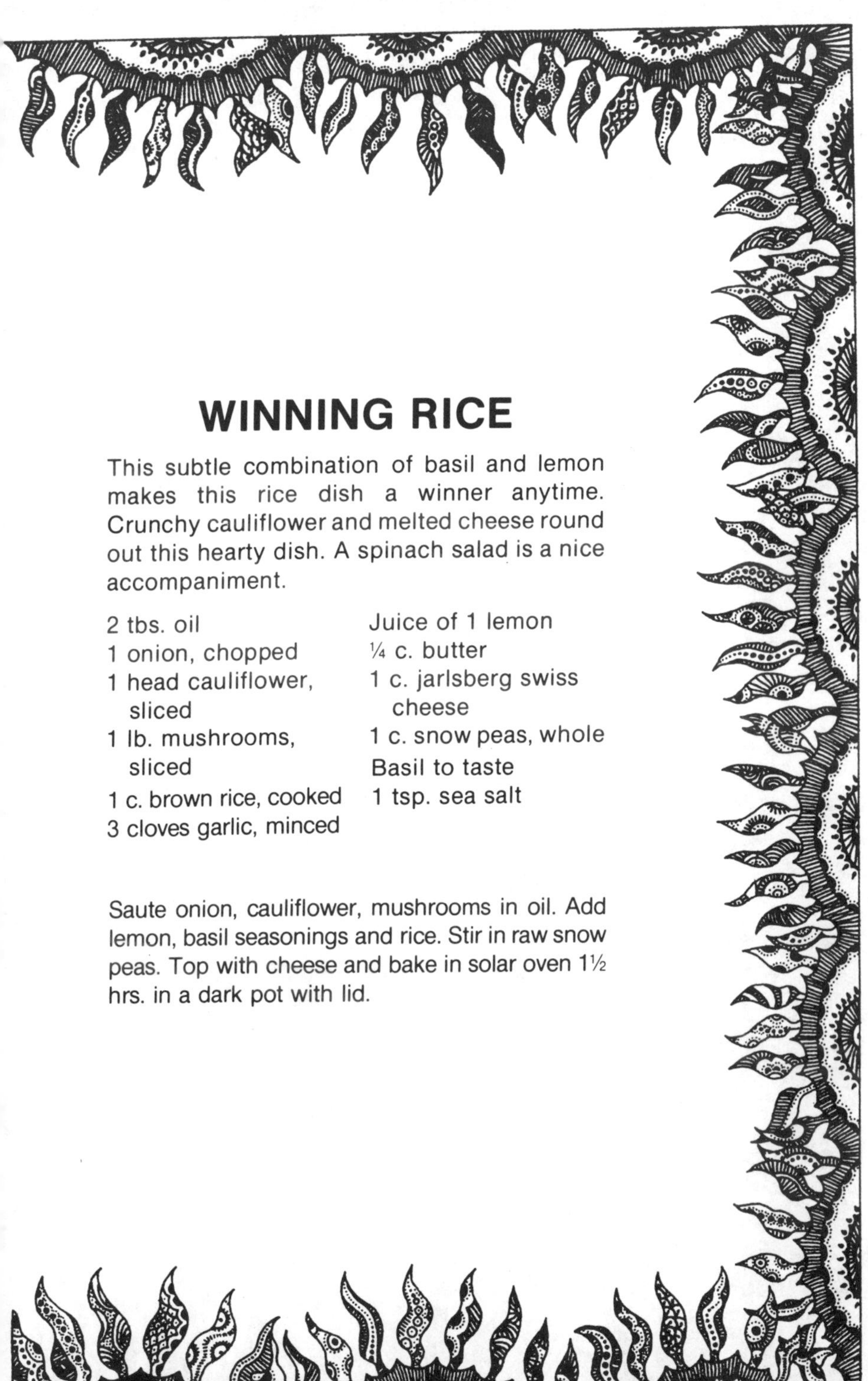

WINNING RICE

This subtle combination of basil and lemon makes this rice dish a winner anytime. Crunchy cauliflower and melted cheese round out this hearty dish. A spinach salad is a nice accompaniment.

2 tbs. oil
1 onion, chopped
1 head cauliflower, sliced
1 lb. mushrooms, sliced
1 c. brown rice, cooked
3 cloves garlic, minced

Juice of 1 lemon
¼ c. butter
1 c. jarlsberg swiss cheese
1 c. snow peas, whole
Basil to taste
1 tsp. sea salt

Saute onion, cauliflower, mushrooms in oil. Add lemon, basil seasonings and rice. Stir in raw snow peas. Top with cheese and bake in solar oven 1½ hrs. in a dark pot with lid.

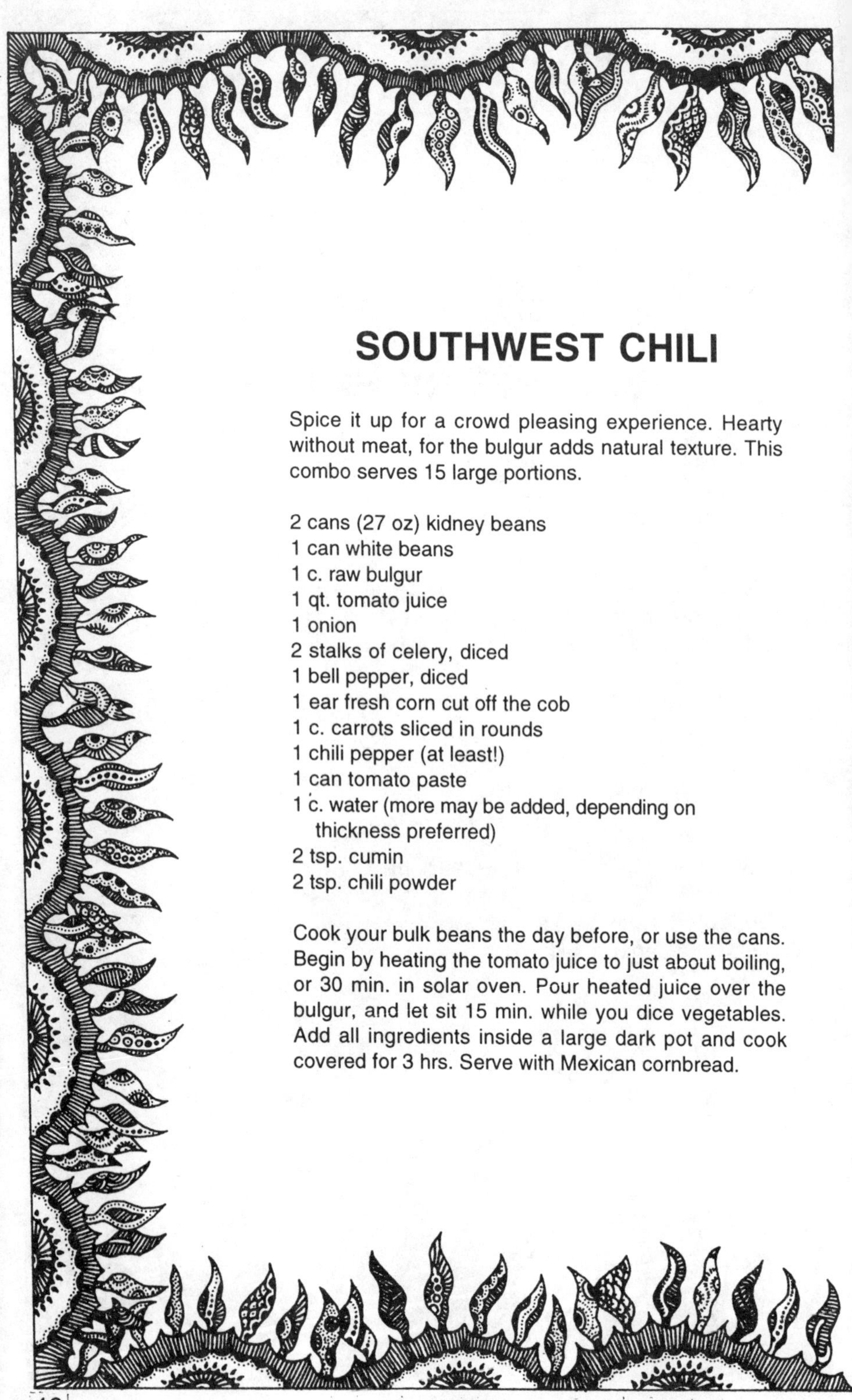

SOUTHWEST CHILI

Spice it up for a crowd pleasing experience. Hearty without meat, for the bulgur adds natural texture. This combo serves 15 large portions.

2 cans (27 oz) kidney beans
1 can white beans
1 c. raw bulgur
1 qt. tomato juice
1 onion
2 stalks of celery, diced
1 bell pepper, diced
1 ear fresh corn cut off the cob
1 c. carrots sliced in rounds
1 chili pepper (at least!)
1 can tomato paste
1 c. water (more may be added, depending on
   thickness preferred)
2 tsp. cumin
2 tsp. chili powder

Cook your bulk beans the day before, or use the cans. Begin by heating the tomato juice to just about boiling, or 30 min. in solar oven. Pour heated juice over the bulgur, and let sit 15 min. while you dice vegetables. Add all ingredients inside a large dark pot and cook covered for 3 hrs. Serve with Mexican cornbread.

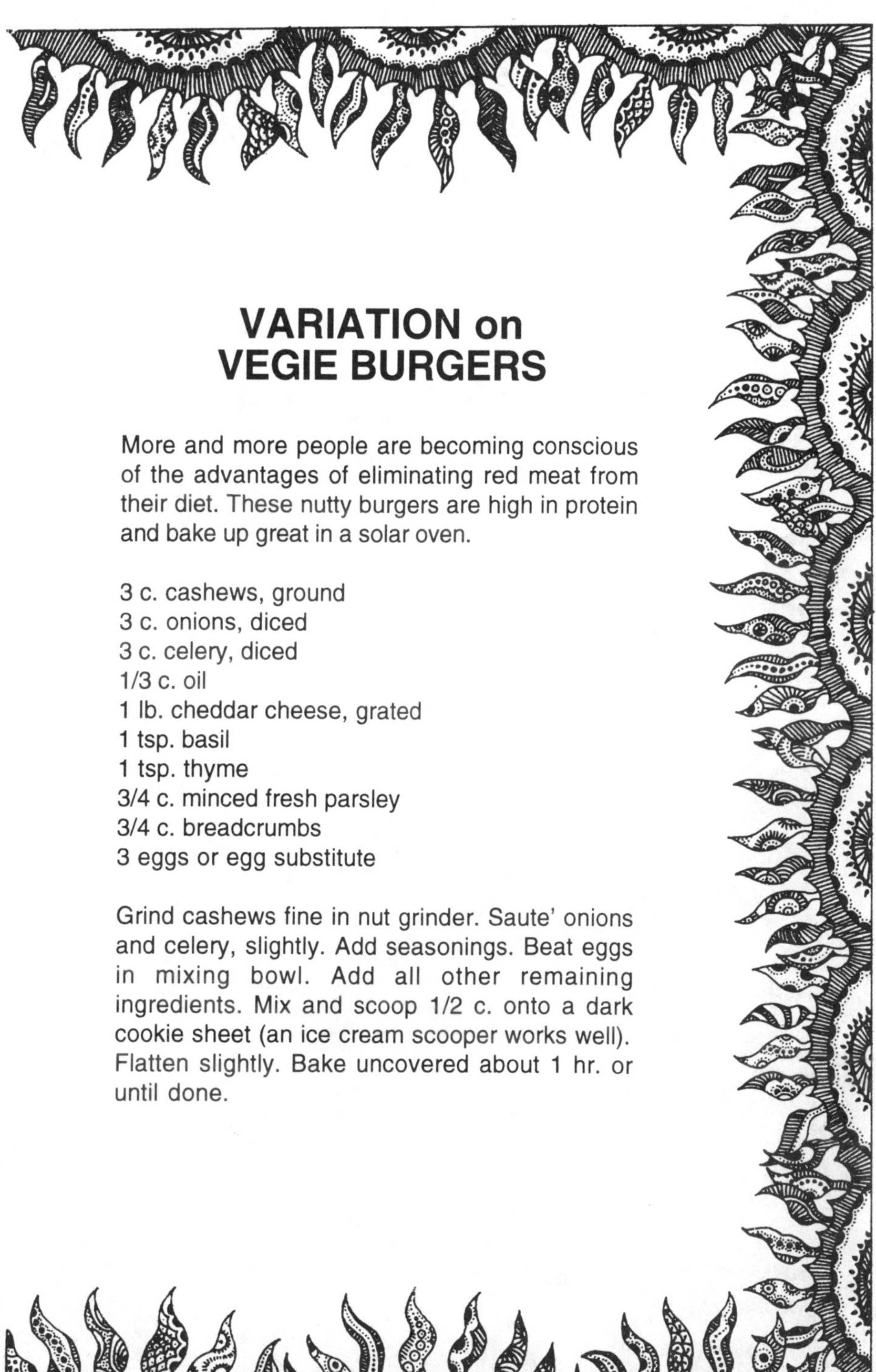

VARIATION on
VEGIE BURGERS

More and more people are becoming conscious of the advantages of eliminating red meat from their diet. These nutty burgers are high in protein and bake up great in a solar oven.

3 c. cashews, ground
3 c. onions, diced
3 c. celery, diced
1/3 c. oil
1 lb. cheddar cheese, grated
1 tsp. basil
1 tsp. thyme
3/4 c. minced fresh parsley
3/4 c. breadcrumbs
3 eggs or egg substitute

Grind cashews fine in nut grinder. Saute' onions and celery, slightly. Add seasonings. Beat eggs in mixing bowl. Add all other remaining ingredients. Mix and scoop 1/2 c. onto a dark cookie sheet (an ice cream scooper works well). Flatten slightly. Bake uncovered about 1 hr. or until done.

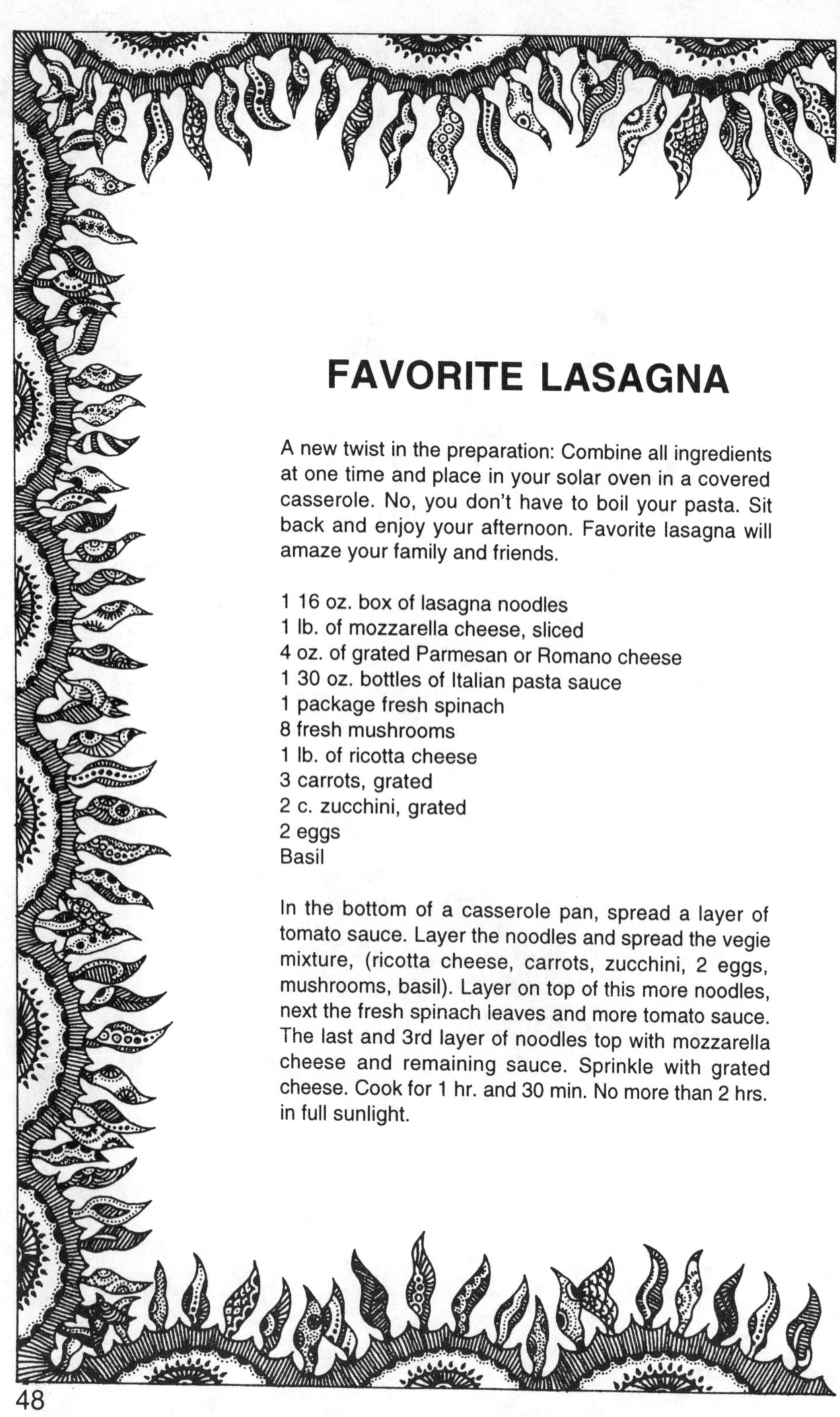

FAVORITE LASAGNA

A new twist in the preparation: Combine all ingredients at one time and place in your solar oven in a covered casserole. No, you don't have to boil your pasta. Sit back and enjoy your afternoon. Favorite lasagna will amaze your family and friends.

1 16 oz. box of lasagna noodles
1 lb. of mozzarella cheese, sliced
4 oz. of grated Parmesan or Romano cheese
1 30 oz. bottles of Italian pasta sauce
1 package fresh spinach
8 fresh mushrooms
1 lb. of ricotta cheese
3 carrots, grated
2 c. zucchini, grated
2 eggs
Basil

In the bottom of a casserole pan, spread a layer of tomato sauce. Layer the noodles and spread the vegie mixture, (ricotta cheese, carrots, zucchini, 2 eggs, mushrooms, basil). Layer on top of this more noodles, next the fresh spinach leaves and more tomato sauce. The last and 3rd layer of noodles top with mozzarella cheese and remaining sauce. Sprinkle with grated cheese. Cook for 1 hr. and 30 min. No more than 2 hrs. in full sunlight.

VEGIE CASSEROLE

Almost a meal in itself nutritionally. Accompany this entree with a green salad.

3½ c. cooked millet
1½ lbs. broccoli,
   steamed, peeled &
   chopped, flowers
   broken up
1 onion, chopped
¾ lbs. mushrooms,
   sliced

3 cloves garlic,
minced
1 tbs. basil
1 tsp. thyme
2½ c. grated Monterey
   Jack cheese

Saute garlic, onions, mushrooms and broccoli gently, about 5 mins. Add herbs. Combine the cooked millet with sauteed vegies and cheese. Turn into amber glassware (2 qt. capacity) and cover with lid. Cook in 250° solar oven for 1 hr.

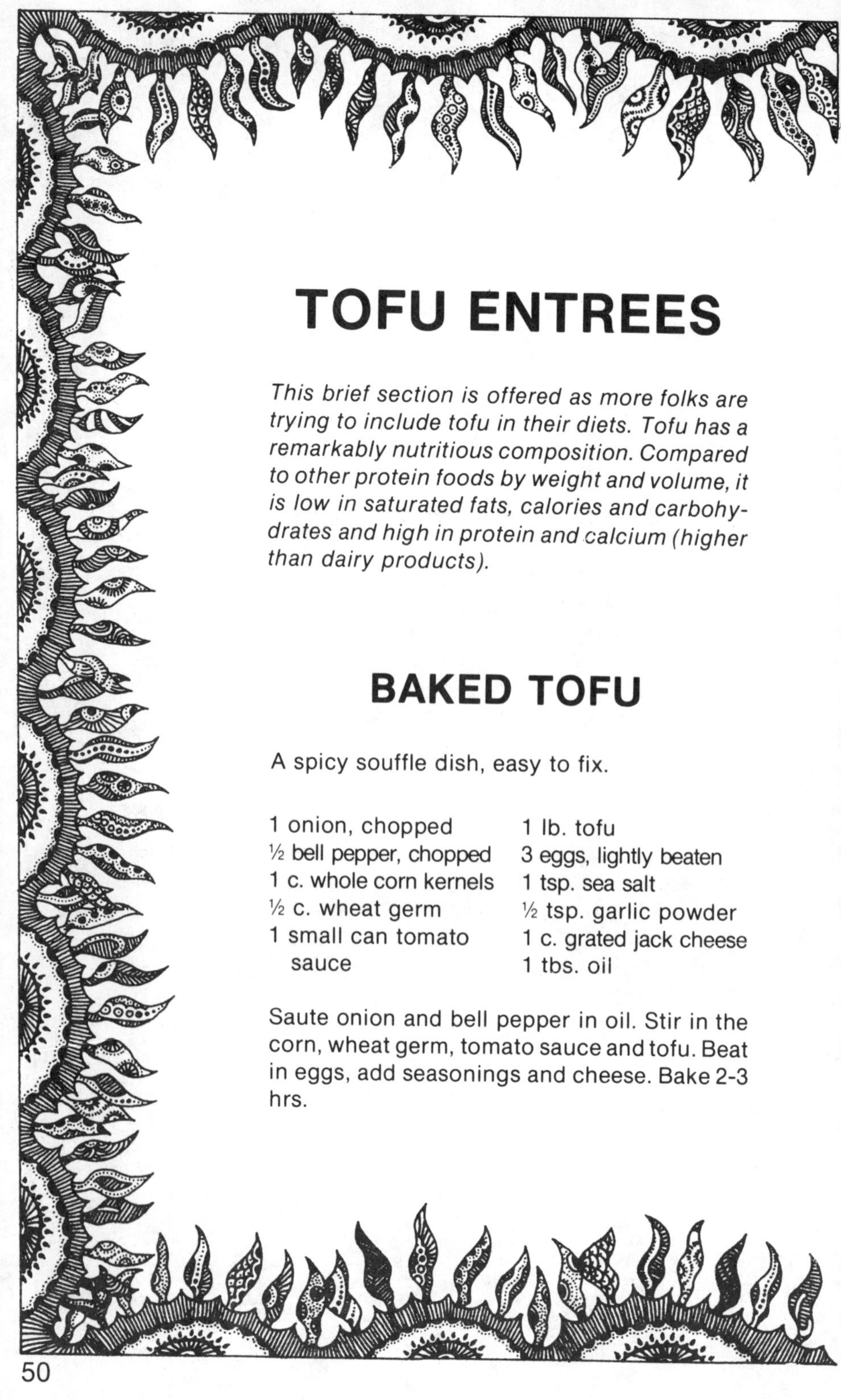

TOFU ENTREES

This brief section is offered as more folks are trying to include tofu in their diets. Tofu has a remarkably nutritious composition. Compared to other protein foods by weight and volume, it is low in saturated fats, calories and carbohydrates and high in protein and calcium (higher than dairy products).

BAKED TOFU

A spicy souffle dish, easy to fix.

1 onion, chopped
½ bell pepper, chopped
1 c. whole corn kernels
½ c. wheat germ
1 small can tomato
   sauce

1 lb. tofu
3 eggs, lightly beaten
1 tsp. sea salt
½ tsp. garlic powder
1 c. grated jack cheese
1 tbs. oil

Saute onion and bell pepper in oil. Stir in the corn, wheat germ, tomato sauce and tofu. Beat in eggs, add seasonings and cheese. Bake 2-3 hrs.

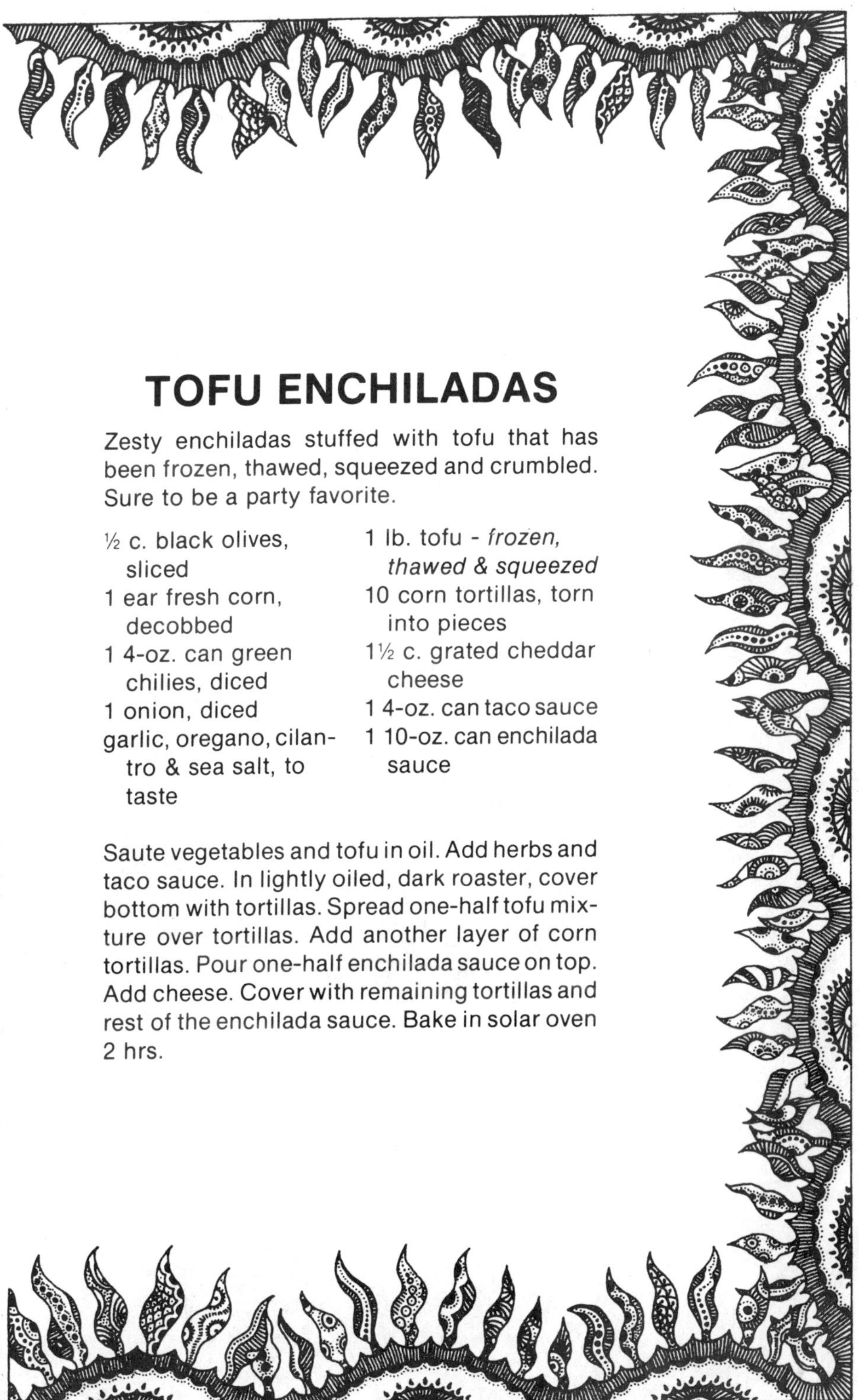

TOFU ENCHILADAS

Zesty enchiladas stuffed with tofu that has been frozen, thawed, squeezed and crumbled. Sure to be a party favorite.

½ c. black olives, sliced

1 ear fresh corn, decobbed

1 4-oz. can green chilies, diced

1 onion, diced

garlic, oregano, cilantro & sea salt, to taste

1 lb. tofu - *frozen, thawed & squeezed*

10 corn tortillas, torn into pieces

1½ c. grated cheddar cheese

1 4-oz. can taco sauce

1 10-oz. can enchilada sauce

Saute vegetables and tofu in oil. Add herbs and taco sauce. In lightly oiled, dark roaster, cover bottom with tortillas. Spread one-half tofu mixture over tortillas. Add another layer of corn tortillas. Pour one-half enchilada sauce on top. Add cheese. Cover with remaining tortillas and rest of the enchilada sauce. Bake in solar oven 2 hrs.

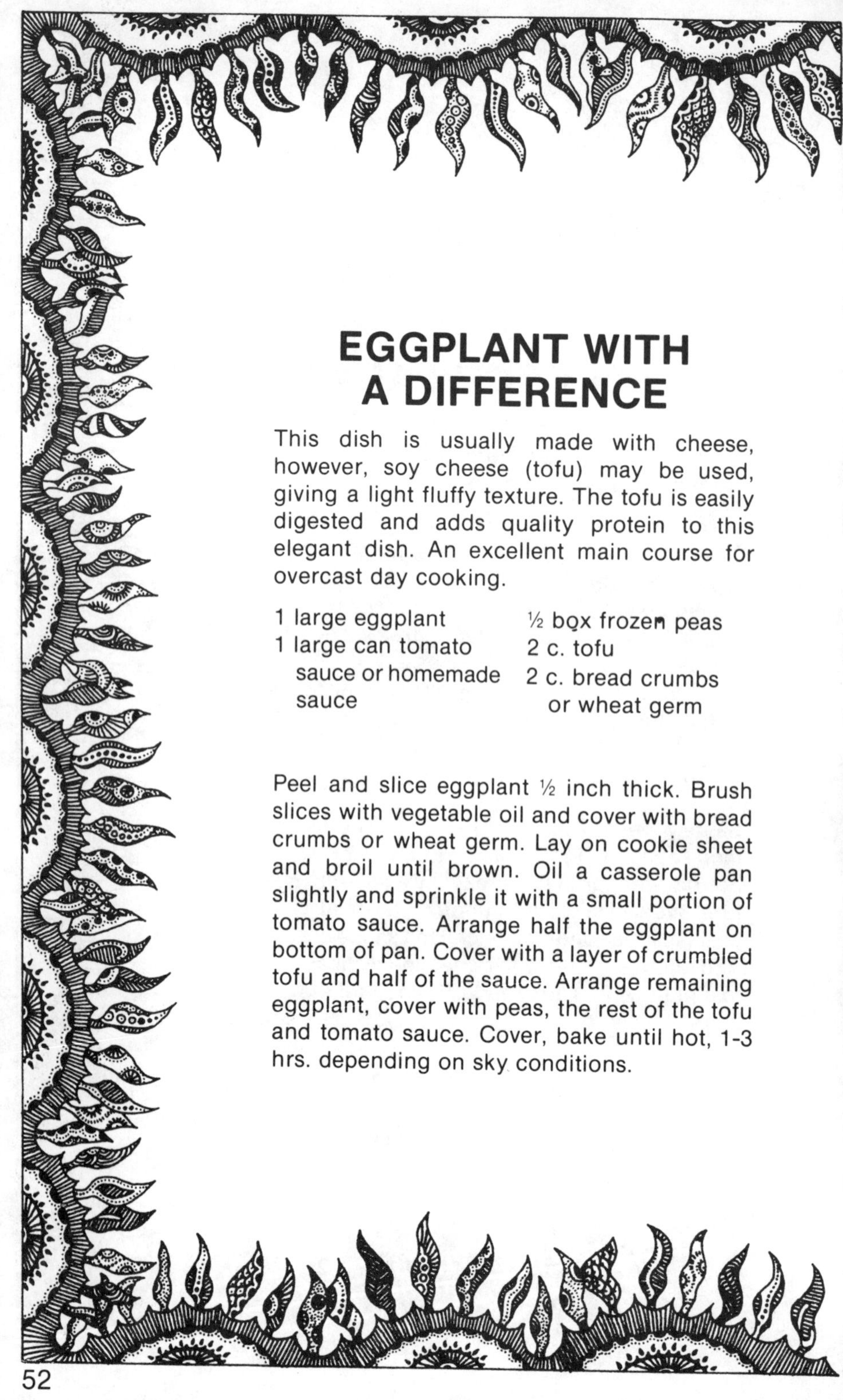

EGGPLANT WITH A DIFFERENCE

This dish is usually made with cheese, however, soy cheese (tofu) may be used, giving a light fluffy texture. The tofu is easily digested and adds quality protein to this elegant dish. An excellent main course for overcast day cooking.

1 large eggplant	½ box frozen peas
1 large can tomato sauce or homemade sauce	2 c. tofu
	2 c. bread crumbs or wheat germ

Peel and slice eggplant ½ inch thick. Brush slices with vegetable oil and cover with bread crumbs or wheat germ. Lay on cookie sheet and broil until brown. Oil a casserole pan slightly and sprinkle it with a small portion of tomato sauce. Arrange half the eggplant on bottom of pan. Cover with a layer of crumbled tofu and half of the sauce. Arrange remaining eggplant, cover with peas, the rest of the tofu and tomato sauce. Cover, bake until hot, 1-3 hrs. depending on sky conditions.

TOFU STEW

Aromatic and robust — this flavorsome stew satisfies a healthy appetite for a cool night's dinner.

1 pk. onion stew mix
  (no preservatives,
  no sugar, no MSG)
1 onion, diced
4 cups of water
2 tbs butter
½ c chianti wine
4 potatoes, chunks
3 carrots, rounds
2 stalks celery, diced
	1 c fresh green beans
	1 bell pepper, diced
	3 tomatoes, chunks
	6-10 mushrooms,
	  sliced
	bunch green tops
	  from beets
	1 lb tofu, bite size
	  pieces

Place all ingredients in large black pot and cover. Simmer in solar oven all day during the winter season.

TOFU CUTLETS

Minutes to prepare, our family's favorite way to enjoy tofu for lunch. Can be eaten alone or between a corn tortilla, nori sheet or whole wheat bun with alfalfa sprouts.

½ lb tofu, cut in ½
  inch cakes
½ c combination
  equal part olive oil
and tamari
	1 tsp ginger powder
	2 cloves garlic,
	  minced
	few sprigs of parsley
	  minced

Make a marinade of all ingredients except the tofu. Sprinkle the tofu with the marinade, cover and bake 1 hour.

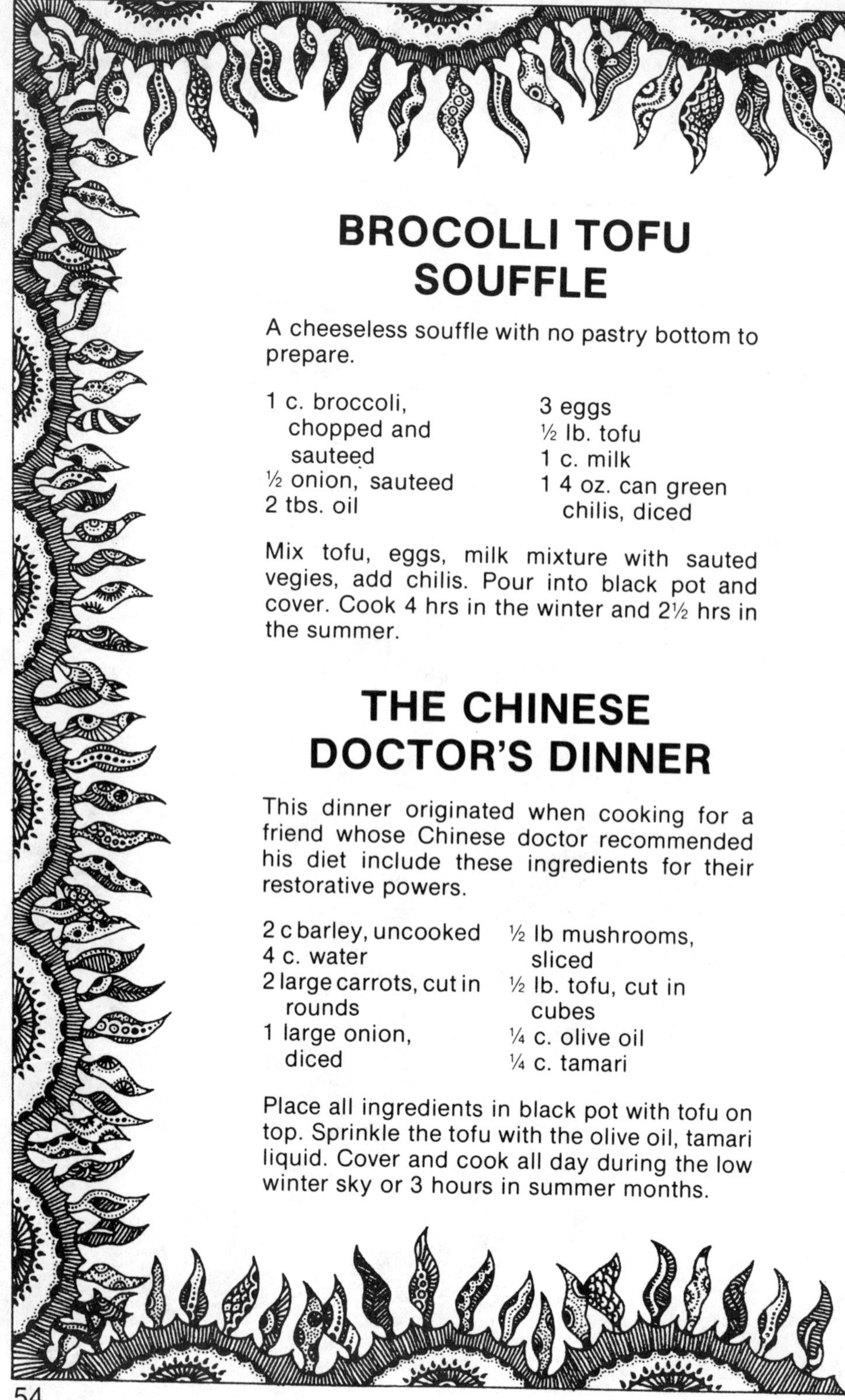

BROCOLLI TOFU SOUFFLE

A cheeseless souffle with no pastry bottom to prepare.

1 c. broccoli,
chopped and
sauteed
½ onion, sauteed
2 tbs. oil

3 eggs
½ lb. tofu
1 c. milk
1 4 oz. can green
chilis, diced

Mix tofu, eggs, milk mixture with sauted vegies, add chilis. Pour into black pot and cover. Cook 4 hrs in the winter and 2½ hrs in the summer.

THE CHINESE DOCTOR'S DINNER

This dinner originated when cooking for a friend whose Chinese doctor recommended his diet include these ingredients for their restorative powers.

2 c barley, uncooked
4 c. water
2 large carrots, cut in
rounds
1 large onion,
diced

½ lb mushrooms,
sliced
½ lb. tofu, cut in
cubes
¼ c. olive oil
¼ c. tamari

Place all ingredients in black pot with tofu on top. Sprinkle the tofu with the olive oil, tamari liquid. Cover and cook all day during the low winter sky or 3 hours in summer months.

TOFU CHEESECAKE

Surprise. My family doesn't recognize that this cheesecake was made of tofu. The range of possibilities for tofu does include desserts and being low in calories what a wonderful way to enjoy treats.

6 solar baked apples
½ lb. tofu
½ c. maple syrup
2 tbs. frozen orange
  juice concentrate
½ tsp. cinnamon
1 tbs. sesame tahini

1 tsp. pure lemon
  extract
3 tbs. arrowroot
  powder
1 c. milk
3 eggs
40 uncooked whole
  cranberries

Bake 6 medium apples as in Saucy Apples. Cool the apples. Core, blend the pulp including the skin. Mix remaining ingredients together and pour into an uncooked *date crust*. Decorate with whole cranberries. This pie cooked on a cool partially cloudy November day in Phoenix, Arizona.

Date Crust

7 graham cracker
  squares, crushed
  into powder
½ c. wheat germ

½ c. whole wheat
  flour
6 tbs butter, soft
8 dates chopped fine

Mix everything together and mould into a 9 inch pie pan.

POULTRY

Solar cooked poultry testifies to the nutritional energy of how natural sunlight cooks and enhances food. Demonstrate the art of solar cooking with the following experiment. Place one chicken cut up with a small amount of liquid, such as lemon juice/tamari combination, inside a dark brown clear glass covered casserole dish. With glass one can see what is cooking. After 2½ hrs. the chicken will be tastefully roasted. But, continue to cook the chicken all afternoon, for six hours. Remove a piece every hour. Test and taste. No other way of cooking could produce such delicious and tender yet unburned food.

SAUCY CHICKEN

Perk chicken up by choosing either picante, curry or barbecue sauce.

1 whole chicken, cut up
1-2 c. sauce, as above

Just cover the chicken with your choice of sauce. Ready to serve in 2½ hrs. or anytime afterwards.

CHICKEN ENCHILADAS

Create a solar Southwestern cuisine. This dish, prepared a day ahead, leaves you fresh for a company dinner.

4 chicken breasts, de-
boned & cooked
12 corn tortillas,
cut in 1" strips
1 can cream of mush-
room soup
1½ c. milk

1 can cream of chicken
soup
1 4-oz. can green
chilies, diced
1-2 c. cheddar cheese,
grated

Cover chicken with water and cook until tender, 2½ hrs. De-bone chicken, reserve stock for soup. In a 9 x 13 pan, pour a little broth and cover with pieces of chicken. Layer with strips of tortilla, another layer of chicken and top with remaining tortilla strips. Make a sauce of the soup, chilies and milk. Pour sauce over the chicken enchiladas and marinate in refrigerator overnight. Place in a preheated solar oven and cook 3 hrs. Sprinkle top with cheese last 20 mins. of cooking.

COQ AU VIN

Impress outdoor barbecue-ers with this skillfully simple dish. Kerr-Cole Eco-Cookers weigh 17 lbs. and are portable for outings.

1 chicken, cut in pieces
1 onion, cut up
2 cloves garlic, crushed
4 carrots, chopped bite-size
½ tsp. thyme
½ tsp. rosemary
1 bay leaf
½ tsp arrowroot powder
2-4 c. red wine (burgundy)

Place everything in a dark roaster and cover. Will be ready to serve in 3 hrs. The sauce created in the cooking process is delicious over solar rice.

CHICKEN & ARTICHOKES

An elegant way to serve chicken.

1 chicken, cut up
¼ lb. fresh mushrooms
¼ c. butter
5 tbs. sherry
1 pkg. frozen artichoke hearts

Place chicken skin side down in a dark roaster. Melt butter and add sherry. Pour over chicken. Arrange artichoke hearts and mushrooms between chicken pieces. Bake 3 hrs

CHICKEN CACCIATTORE

Italian-style chicken lends a homey elegance to a meal.

1 chicken, cut up
1 onion, chopped
2 8-oz. cans tomato
  sauce
1 16-oz. can whole
  tomatoes
1 tsp. oregano
1 tsp. thyme
1 tsp. basil
1 tsp. sea salt

3 cloves garlic,
  minced
¼ c. red cooking
  wine
2 c. fresh mushrooms,
  sliced
½ c. parmesan cheese
¼ c. fresh parsley
  chopped fine

Preheat solar oven. Mix all ingredients except chicken in large, dark-colored baking pan. Add chicken pieces and cover thoroughly with sauce. Cover and bake 4-5 hrs. Baking chicken longer will not burn it. Garnish with parsley on bed of solar rice. Sprinkle parmesan cheese on top when serving.

CHICKEN GUMBO

The Southern Belle of chicken dishes features okra, which thickens the broth.

1 large stewing chicken	1 large onion, chopped
1 qt. water	2 c. okra, cut in rounds
1 tsp. sea salt	1 large can whole
1 tsp. thyme	tomatoes
4 c. corn kernels	2 c. baby lima beans

Solar cook chicken 3 hrs. Cut cooked chicken in 2" pieces. Add all the vegetables and chicken pieces to the chicken stock. Cook, covered, in dark pot 3 hrs.

MARINATED TURKEY TENDERS

Delicious simplicity! The tenderloins can be marinated and refrigerated the night before, or up to 2 hrs. before solar cooking time.

1-2 lbs. of fresh turkey tenderloins

Marinade:

1/4 c. olive oil
juice of one lemon
1 tsp. oregano
1 tsp. garlic powder

Place turkey in roasting bag with marinade. Refrigerate. Bake in solar oven about 2 1/2 hours or until ready to serve.

WELL SEASONED TURKEY

Set aglow with solar cooking and chili powder, a traditional turkey breast transforms conventional tastes.

1 fresh turkey breast, salted & peppered
1 lemon
1 tbs. olive oil
Sprig of fresh thyme
1 bay leaf
3 cloves of garlic
1 tbs. chili powder
1 onion, quartered
4 stalks of celery
2 carrots

Coat turkey with lemon juice and olive oil. Tuck under the breast the thyme, bay leaf and garlic. Set around the sides the quartered onion, celery sticks and carrot slices. Pat the breast with chili powder. Cook 4 to 5 hours. Ladle the broth over your favorite stuffing.

CILANTRO CHICKEN

Skinless chicken sparked with the delectable herb, cilantro, is a delicious low-fat dish that goes well with Spanish rice or a zita pasta.

10 large chicken thighs, skin removed
1 yellow onion, chopped
4 large garlic cloves, minced
1 28 oz. can of crushed tomatoes
2 tbs. red wine vinegar
1 tsp. cumin
several dashes of a hot pepper sauce
1/2 c. chopped fresh cilantro

Put all ingredients into a darkened pot with lid. Let simmer in sun about 3 hrs. or until chicken is cooked through. Pour sauce over rice or pasta.

WHEAT GERM CHICKEN

Who needs to fry chicken when it tastes this good coated with tarragon flavored wheat germ?

8 skinless thighs
2 tsp. tarragon
1 tsp. lemon rind
1 c. wheat germ
1/4 c. milk

Dip thighs in milk so the coating of wheat germ, tarragon and lemon rind stick to the surface of the chicken. Place pieces in a shallow dish. Bake for 3 hours uncovered to achieve a crispy effect.

A SOUTHERN CORNBREAD DRESSING

For stuffing any bird, this is my favorite choice.

6 c. crumbled cornbread, solar cooked
4 c. bread crumbs (whole wheat, 7 grain, etc.)
1 1/2 c. milk
2 onions, chopped
1 c. celery, chopped
6 tbs. butter
4 eggs, well beaten (egg substitute works)
1 tsp. basil
2 tsp. sea salt
1 tsp. black pepper
3 c. vegetable or poultry stock
1/8 tsp. powdered allspice
1/2 tsp. thyme
1/2 tsp. garlic powder

Soak the previously solar cooked cornbread with the bread crumbs in the milk. Saute' the onions and celery in butter until soft. Combine the breads with the sauteed vegetables. Mix and add the eggs. Stir in the seasonings and stock. Bake in solar oven about 2 hrs.

FISH

When cooking fish, a common complaint from the kitchen is the odors they provide. But this need not be with a solar oven.

CASSEROLE OF FISH FILLETS

Fish cooks quickly, without elaborate recipes.

3 fillets of fish
½ c. wheat germ
½ tsp. sea salt
juice of one lemon
½ c. chopped green
onions

Place fish in oiled casserole, sprinkle with wheat germ and chopped green onions. Dot fish with butter, squeeze on lemon juice. (If frozen fish is used no liquid is required.)

TAMARI RED SNAPPER

The tamari sauce transforms red snapper into a dining experience.

3 medium fresh red
snapper fillets
3 cloves garlic, minced
5 fresh tomatoes, cubed
4 tbs. butter
1 tbs. honey
1 tbs. nutritional yeast
1 tsp. arrowroot flour
1½ tsp. tamari, to taste
pinch cayenne pepper

Mince garlic and saute in butter until tender. Add tomatoes, tamari, honey, yeast and cayenne. Place fish in sauce and solar cook approx. 1 hr. Needs to be watched as fish can become flaky if cooked too long.

CORN OYSTER CASSEROLE

An unusual and tasty combination results when fresh oysters meet creamed corn.

2 cans creamed corn
1 pt. fresh oysters, drained & cut up
2 eggs
1 c. milk
crackers to thicken
1 tbs. butter
sea salt, to taste

Combine creamed corn, oysters, eggs and milk. Melt butter to coat sides of baking pan. Thicken oyster mixture with cracker crumbs. Bake approx. 3-4 hrs. in preheated solar oven. Test by putting toothpick in center. If it comes out clean, it is done.

TUNA CASSEROLE

This dish is a favorite with hard-to-please teenagers and a great protein booster. Adding a touch of curry is an optional taste experiment.

1 medium can tuna
2 c. whole grain noodles, cooked
1 c. peas
½ c. onion, chopped
1 c. grated Jarlsberg or other hard cheese
¾ c. milk
2 tbs. butter
2 tbs. whole wheat flour
½ tsp. tarragon
dash cayenne
sea salt
1 or 2 cloves garlic, mashed
½ tsp. basil

Melt butter, add garlic and herbs to pan. Add flour to make paste. Stir in milk until mixture thickens. Combine remaining ingredients in casserole. Pour sauce over all. Bake 2 hrs.

CRAB TART

For special occasions, a crabmeat tart is a worthy choice. Set in a prebaked whole wheat pie crust, this flavorful combination of dill-scented crab can be thinly sliced and savored.

1 tbs. vegetable oil
1 c. mushrooms, sliced
1 tsp. lemon juice
1½ tsp. dried dill
1-1½ c. crab meat
1 pre-baked pie shell

1½ c. half & half milk
3 eggs
½ stick butter, melted
6 tbs. parmesan cheese
1 tbs. fresh parsley, chopped

Saute mushrooms in oil with lemon juice. Add dill and stir in crabmeat. Set aside. Whisk the half & half, eggs, melted butter and parmesan together. Add crabmeat mixture and pour into a pre-baked pie shell. Cook about 3 hrs. until set.

JAMBALAYA

In summer months of solar cooking eliminate saute time and mix everything together. The addition of okra makes *Jambalaya* distinctive.

2 tbs. oil
1 tbs. whole wheat flour
½ c. onion, chopped
1 clove garlic, minced
1 c. canned tomatoes
½ c. water
1 bellpepper, cut fine
¼ tsp. cayenne pepper
¼ tsp. thyme

2 tbs. parsley
1 tbs. Worcestershire sauce
3 c. cooked brown rice
1 c. cooked chicken, diced
1 c. cooked shrimp
1 c. tomato sauce
2 c. okra rounds
1 clove garlic, minced

Everything can be mixed at once. A bit of curry adds another dimension to this recipe. Bake in preheated solar oven 4 hrs.

RAINBOW TROUT

Solar cooking trout retains the rainbow on the skin of the fresh fish.

1 fresh trout, rinsed (frozen fish is acceptable)

Clean and rinse fish. Place trout over a cake rack. Oven needs to be 250 degrees. Lay the trout exposed on rack for 20 min. Turn and cook about 10 min. more or until the juice from the fish is visible.

GARLIC FISH

Try this for brunch.

1 lb. fish fillets cut in
  bite size pieces
1/2 c. butter
4 cloves garlic,
  minced
2 tbs. cooking sherry

1/2 c. wheat germ
1 tsp. fresh parsley,
  minced
1/4 tsp. garlic powder
1 tsp. dry mustard

Melt butter and saute garlic. To garlic butter, add sherry and fish. Saute two minutes. Mix together wheat germ, parsley, garlic powder and dry mustard. To this mixture add 2 tsp. of the garlic butter and stir until moistened. Arrange bite size fish and butter in shallow baking pan and sprinkle with wheat germ. Allow 1 hr. in pre-heated solar oven.

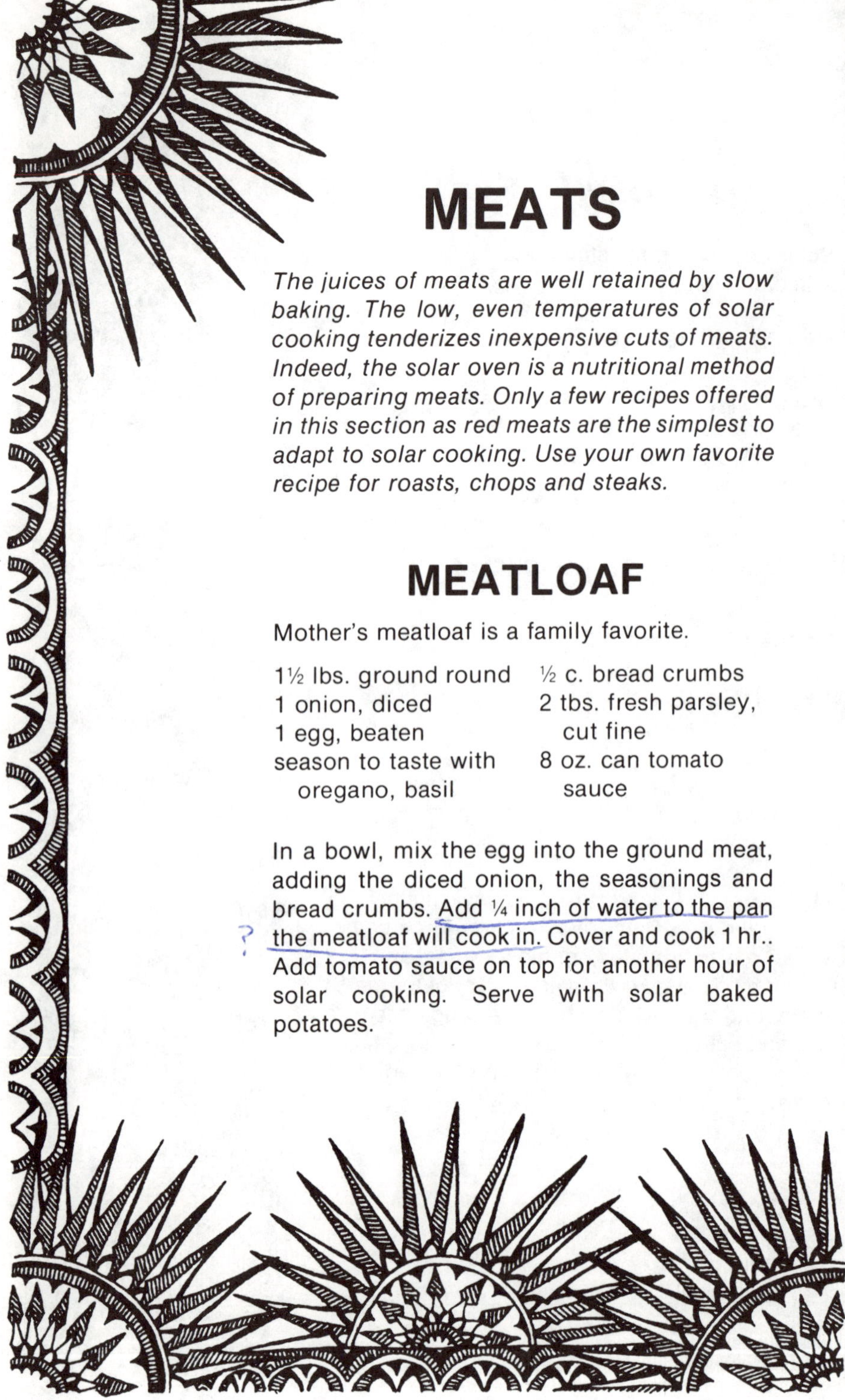

MEATS

The juices of meats are well retained by slow baking. The low, even temperatures of solar cooking tenderizes inexpensive cuts of meats. Indeed, the solar oven is a nutritional method of preparing meats. Only a few recipes offered in this section as red meats are the simplest to adapt to solar cooking. Use your own favorite recipe for roasts, chops and steaks.

MEATLOAF

Mother's meatloaf is a family favorite.

1½ lbs. ground round
1 onion, diced
1 egg, beaten
season to taste with
  oregano, basil

½ c. bread crumbs
2 tbs. fresh parsley,
  cut fine
8 oz. can tomato
  sauce

In a bowl, mix the egg into the ground meat, adding the diced onion, the seasonings and bread crumbs. Add ¼ inch of water to the pan the meatloaf will cook in. Cover and cook 1 hr.. Add tomato sauce on top for another hour of solar cooking. Serve with solar baked potatoes.

SUN STEW

Solar cooking is ideal for stewing meats. You can forego dredging it in flour and browning in oil. You can't overcook sun stew, so enjoy time away from "timing." To serve for dinner, place in solar oven before noon.

2 lbs. lamb or beef cubes	2 potatoes, cut up
water & tomato juice, to cover meat	2 carrots, cut up
3 stalks celery, cut up	1 c. mushrooms
	thyme to season

Combine everything in dark roaster and cover. Cook 4-6 hrs.

ROASTS

Roasts baked 3 to 4 hrs. at low temperatures get very tender, keep moist and brown nicely. Place roast in oiled dark roaster. Add ¼ c. water, cover and cook up to 4 hrs. or more, depending on size of roast and how often you wish to adjust cooker to maximum sunlight.

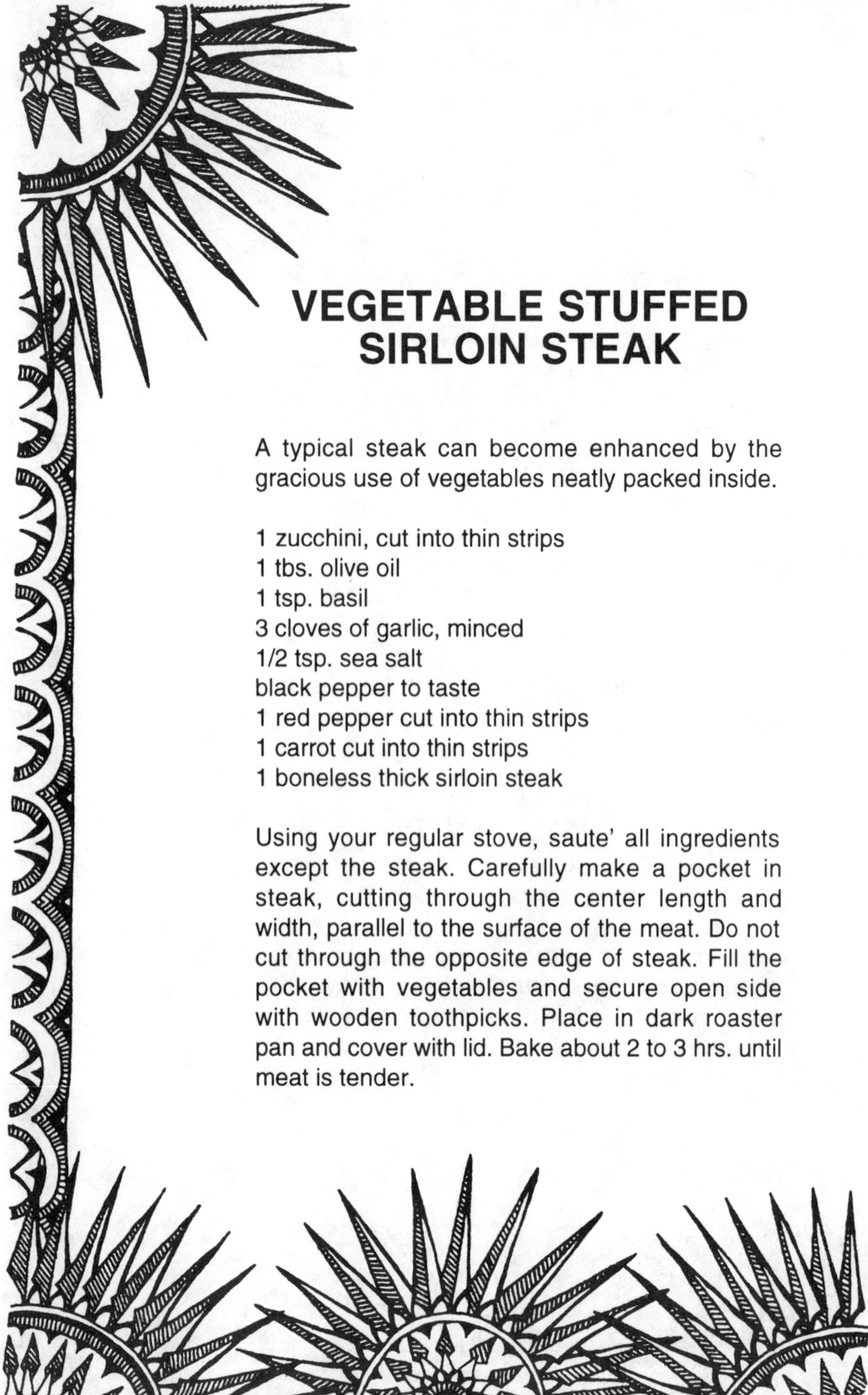

VEGETABLE STUFFED SIRLOIN STEAK

A typical steak can become enhanced by the gracious use of vegetables neatly packed inside.

1 zucchini, cut into thin strips
1 tbs. olive oil
1 tsp. basil
3 cloves of garlic, minced
1/2 tsp. sea salt
black pepper to taste
1 red pepper cut into thin strips
1 carrot cut into thin strips
1 boneless thick sirloin steak

Using your regular stove, saute' all ingredients except the steak. Carefully make a pocket in steak, cutting through the center length and width, parallel to the surface of the meat. Do not cut through the opposite edge of steak. Fill the pocket with vegetables and secure open side with wooden toothpicks. Place in dark roaster pan and cover with lid. Bake about 2 to 3 hrs. until meat is tender.

BEEF STROGANOFF

The cheaper cuts of meat become tender morsels when sun cooked. Serve with noodles *al dente*. Always cook noodles on top of conventional stove.

1½ lbs. bite size beef cubes

2 cloves garlic, minced

½ c. onion, sliced

1 c. fresh mushrooms

1 c. beef broth

1 c. sour cream

Place **all** ingredients except sour cream in dark covered pot. Cook 3 hrs. Stir in 1 c. sour cream 10 minutes before serving over spinach noodles.

PORCUPINES

These make lovely appetizers, with a toothpick in the middle of each one, for serving to guests.

1 lb. ground beef

1 tbs. onion, minced

¾ c. milk

½ c. long grain rice

2 cans tomato soup

Form into small balls and place in a roaster pot. Cover with 2 cans of tomato soup. Bake 2½ hrs. in solar oven with lid on.

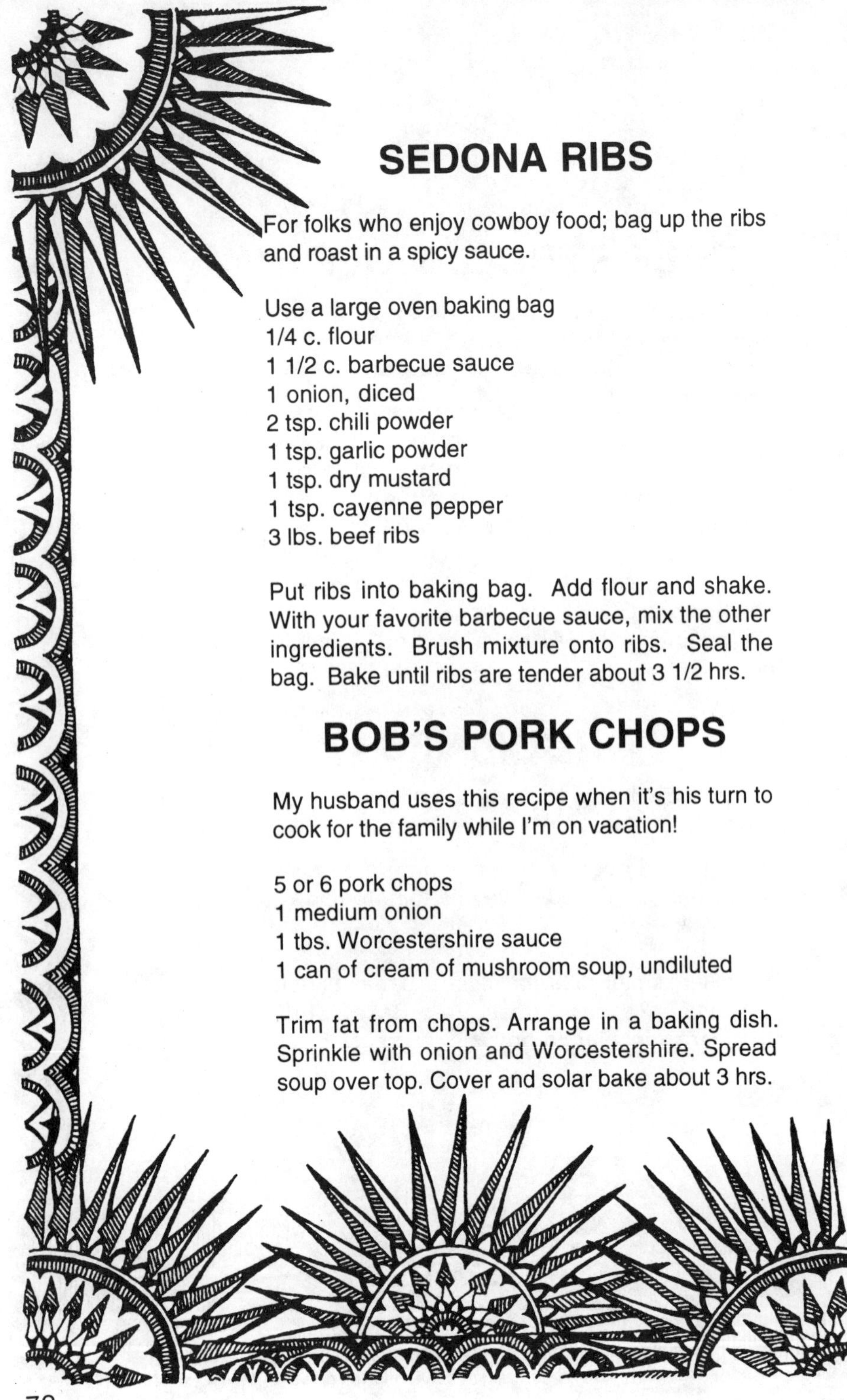

SEDONA RIBS

For folks who enjoy cowboy food; bag up the ribs
and roast in a spicy sauce.

Use a large oven baking bag
1/4 c. flour
1 1/2 c. barbecue sauce
1 onion, diced
2 tsp. chili powder
1 tsp. garlic powder
1 tsp. dry mustard
1 tsp. cayenne pepper
3 lbs. beef ribs

Put ribs into baking bag. Add flour and shake.
With your favorite barbecue sauce, mix the other
ingredients. Brush mixture onto ribs. Seal the
bag. Bake until ribs are tender about 3 1/2 hrs.

BOB'S PORK CHOPS

My husband uses this recipe when it's his turn to
cook for the family while I'm on vacation!

5 or 6 pork chops
1 medium onion
1 tbs. Worcestershire sauce
1 can of cream of mushroom soup, undiluted

Trim fat from chops. Arrange in a baking dish.
Sprinkle with onion and Worcestershire. Spread
soup over top. Cover and solar bake about 3 hrs.

BEEF FAJITAS

Enjoy fajitas without frying the meat in hot oil.

1 large onion, sliced
1 red bell pepper, thinly sliced
1/4 tsp. cumin
1/4 tsp. chili powder
1/4 tsp. cayenne pepper
1 tsp. garlic powder
1/4 tsp. oregano
1/4 tsp. thyme
1/2 c. bouillon broth
1 lb. thinly sliced beef

Lightly flour inside of a roasting bag. Add sliced onion, the slices of red pepper, seasonings, 1/2 c. bouillon broth and the thin strips of beef. Tie the roasting bag and solar bake up to 3 or 4 hrs. Spoon cooked mixture warmed onto flour tortillas. Top with chopped tomato, avocado and salsa.

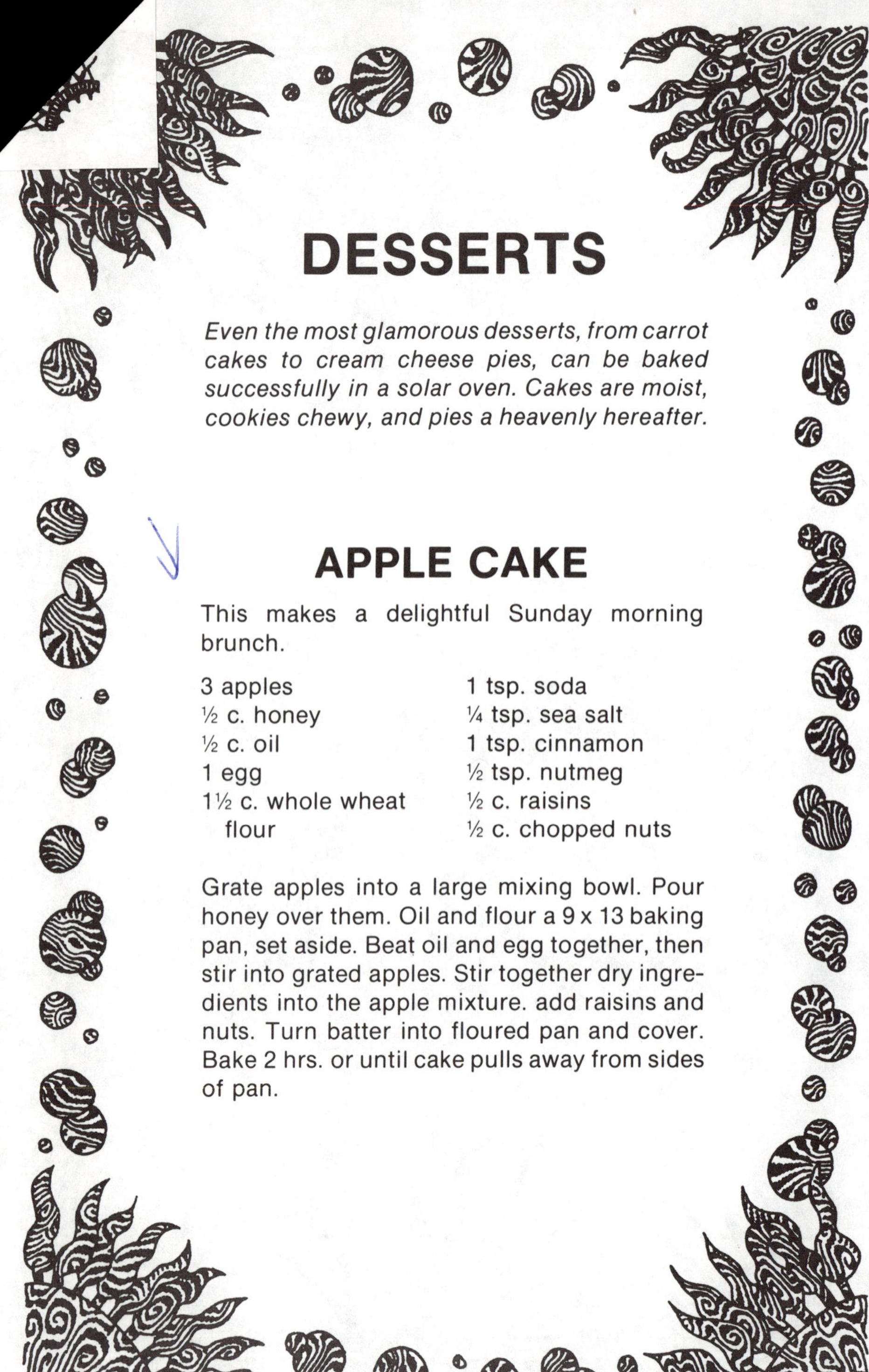

DESSERTS

Even the most glamorous desserts, from carrot cakes to cream cheese pies, can be baked successfully in a solar oven. Cakes are moist, cookies chewy, and pies a heavenly hereafter.

APPLE CAKE

This makes a delightful Sunday morning brunch.

3 apples	1 tsp. soda
½ c. honey	¼ tsp. sea salt
½ c. oil	1 tsp. cinnamon
1 egg	½ tsp. nutmeg
1½ c. whole wheat flour	½ c. raisins
	½ c. chopped nuts

Grate apples into a large mixing bowl. Pour honey over them. Oil and flour a 9 x 13 baking pan, set aside. Beat oil and egg together, then stir into grated apples. Stir together dry ingredients into the apple mixture. add raisins and nuts. Turn batter into floured pan and cover. Bake 2 hrs. or until cake pulls away from sides of pan.

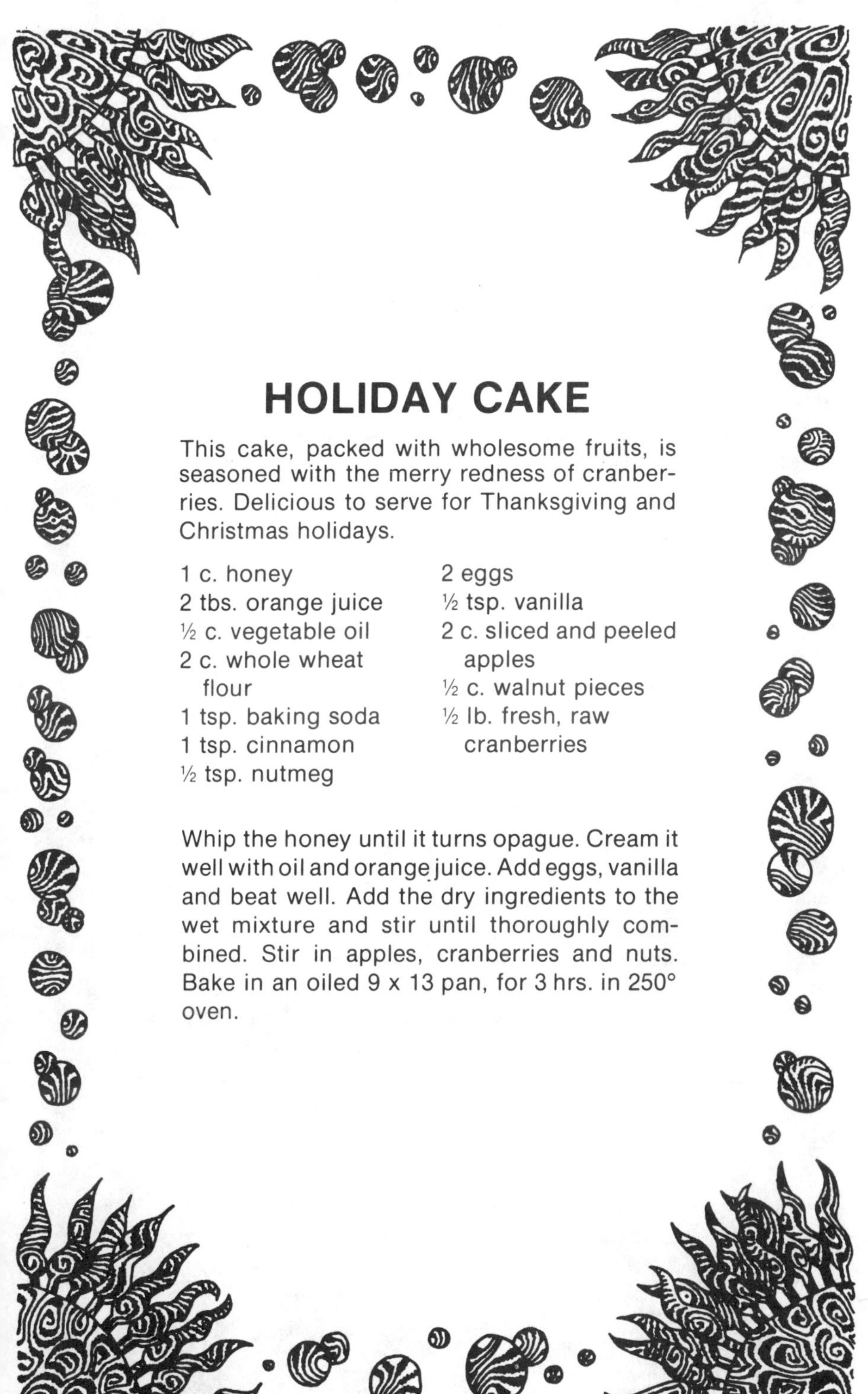

HOLIDAY CAKE

This cake, packed with wholesome fruits, is seasoned with the merry redness of cranberries. Delicious to serve for Thanksgiving and Christmas holidays.

1 c. honey
2 tbs. orange juice
½ c. vegetable oil
2 c. whole wheat
  flour
1 tsp. baking soda
1 tsp. cinnamon
½ tsp. nutmeg

2 eggs
½ tsp. vanilla
2 c. sliced and peeled
  apples
½ c. walnut pieces
½ lb. fresh, raw
  cranberries

Whip the honey until it turns opague. Cream it well with oil and orange juice. Add eggs, vanilla and beat well. Add the dry ingredients to the wet mixture and stir until thoroughly combined. Stir in apples, cranberries and nuts. Bake in an oiled 9 x 13 pan, for 3 hrs. in 250° oven.

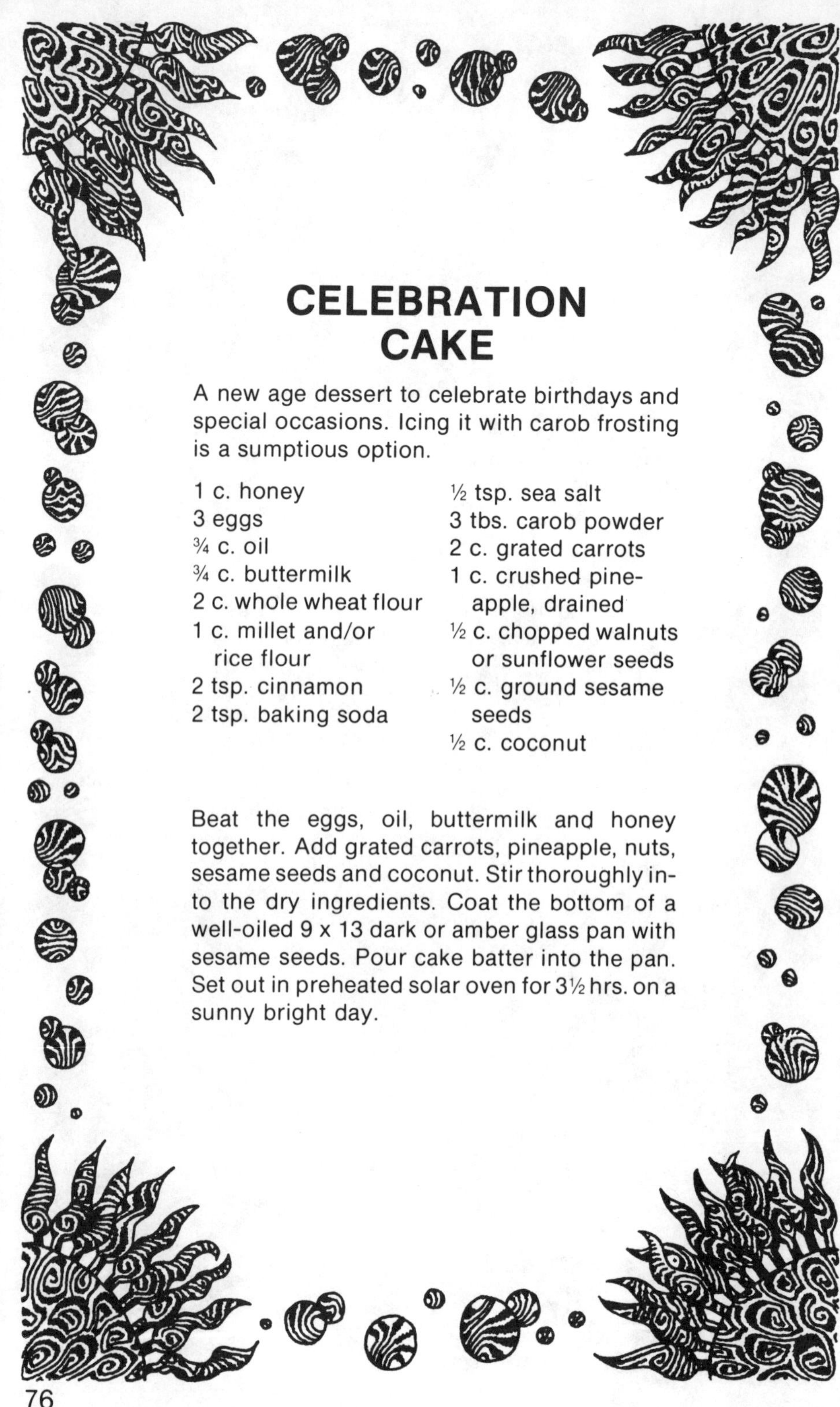

CELEBRATION CAKE

A new age dessert to celebrate birthdays and special occasions. Icing it with carob frosting is a sumptious option.

1 c. honey
3 eggs
¾ c. oil
¾ c. buttermilk
2 c. whole wheat flour
1 c. millet and/or rice flour
2 tsp. cinnamon
2 tsp. baking soda
½ tsp. sea salt
3 tbs. carob powder
2 c. grated carrots
1 c. crushed pineapple, drained
½ c. chopped walnuts or sunflower seeds
½ c. ground sesame seeds
½ c. coconut

Beat the eggs, oil, buttermilk and honey together. Add grated carrots, pineapple, nuts, sesame seeds and coconut. Stir thoroughly into the dry ingredients. Coat the bottom of a well-oiled 9 x 13 dark or amber glass pan with sesame seeds. Pour cake batter into the pan. Set out in preheated solar oven for 3½ hrs. on a sunny bright day.

FRENCH POPPYSEED CAKE

Good French bakers insist on separating the eggs to make delicious cakes.

½ c. butter	1 tsp. baking powder
1 c. honey	¾ tsp. baking soda
4 eggs	¼ tsp. sea salt
2½ c. whole wheat flour	¾ c. buttermilk
	1 grated orange rind

Cream butter and honey together. Add egg yolks, salt and orange peel. Add alternately, flour sifted with baking powder, soda and buttermilk. Beat egg whites until stiff peaks form. Incorporate into the batter together with the poppyseeds, *delicately.* Pour into buttered and floured pan. Sprinkle with poppyseeds and bake until golden brown on top, 2-3 hrs.

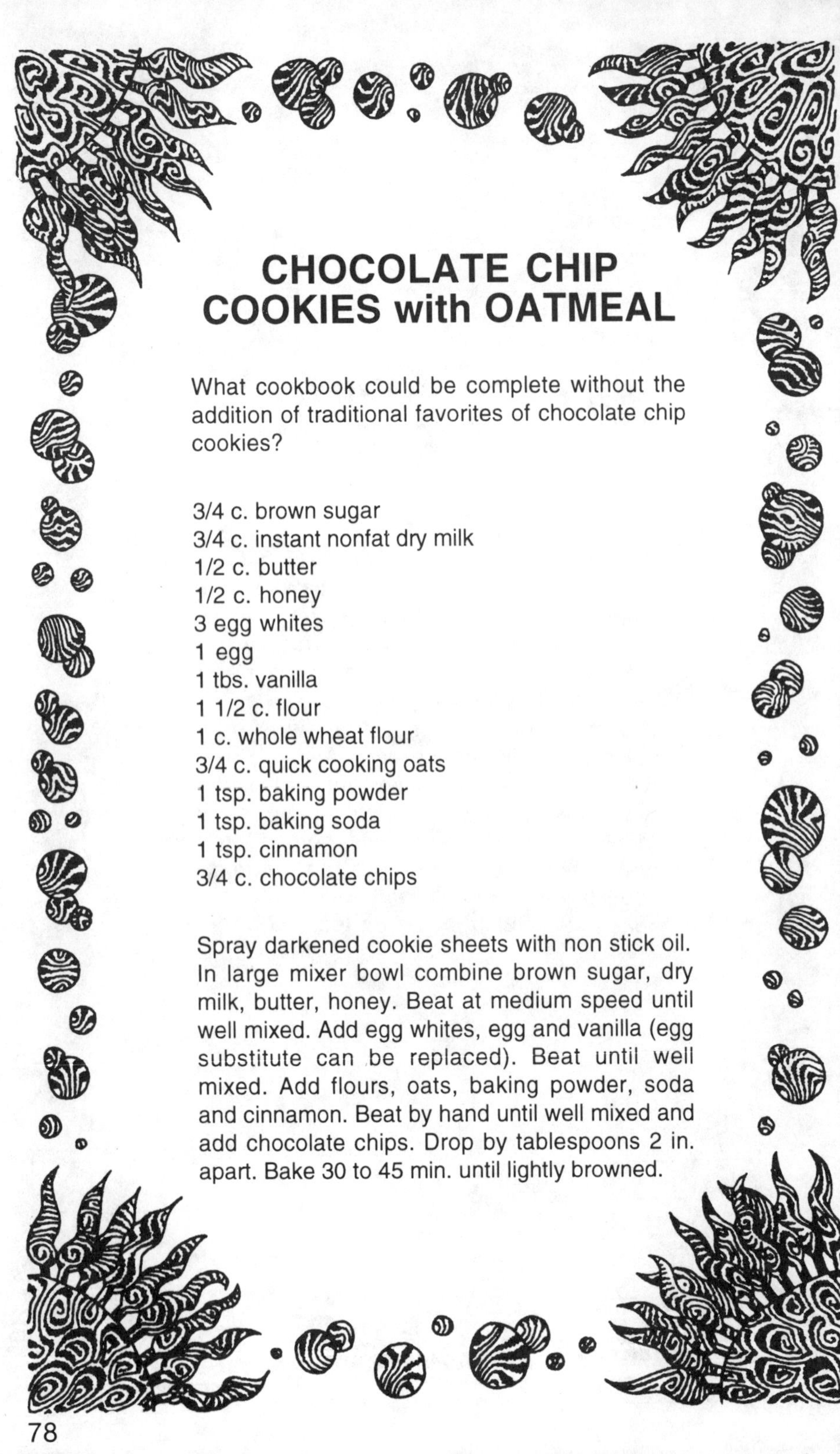

CHOCOLATE CHIP
COOKIES with OATMEAL

What cookbook could be complete without the addition of traditional favorites of chocolate chip cookies?

3/4 c. brown sugar
3/4 c. instant nonfat dry milk
1/2 c. butter
1/2 c. honey
3 egg whites
1 egg
1 tbs. vanilla
1 1/2 c. flour
1 c. whole wheat flour
3/4 c. quick cooking oats
1 tsp. baking powder
1 tsp. baking soda
1 tsp. cinnamon
3/4 c. chocolate chips

Spray darkened cookie sheets with non stick oil. In large mixer bowl combine brown sugar, dry milk, butter, honey. Beat at medium speed until well mixed. Add egg whites, egg and vanilla (egg substitute can be replaced). Beat until well mixed. Add flours, oats, baking powder, soda and cinnamon. Beat by hand until well mixed and add chocolate chips. Drop by tablespoons 2 in. apart. Bake 30 to 45 min. until lightly browned.

SUNNY BROWNIES

One taste and you wish you had made more of these treats.

1½ c. whole wheat flour
¼ tsp. sea salt
½ c. butter
½ c. carob powder
¾ c. honey
3 eggs, well beaten
2/3 c. broken pecans
1 drop peppermint oil
1-2 tsp. milk, to thin batter, if needed

Stir together flour and salt. Melt butter in small saucepan over low heat. Add carob powder and honey; blend and remove from heat. In mixing bowl, beat eggs well, gradually add carob mixtue. Add dry ingredients and mix well by hand. Blend in nuts and peppermint oil. Pour into well-oiled, 8-inch-square pan. Bake in solar oven approx. 45 mins. or until toothpick inserted comes out clean. In winter months or overcast days this dessert may take 3 hrs.

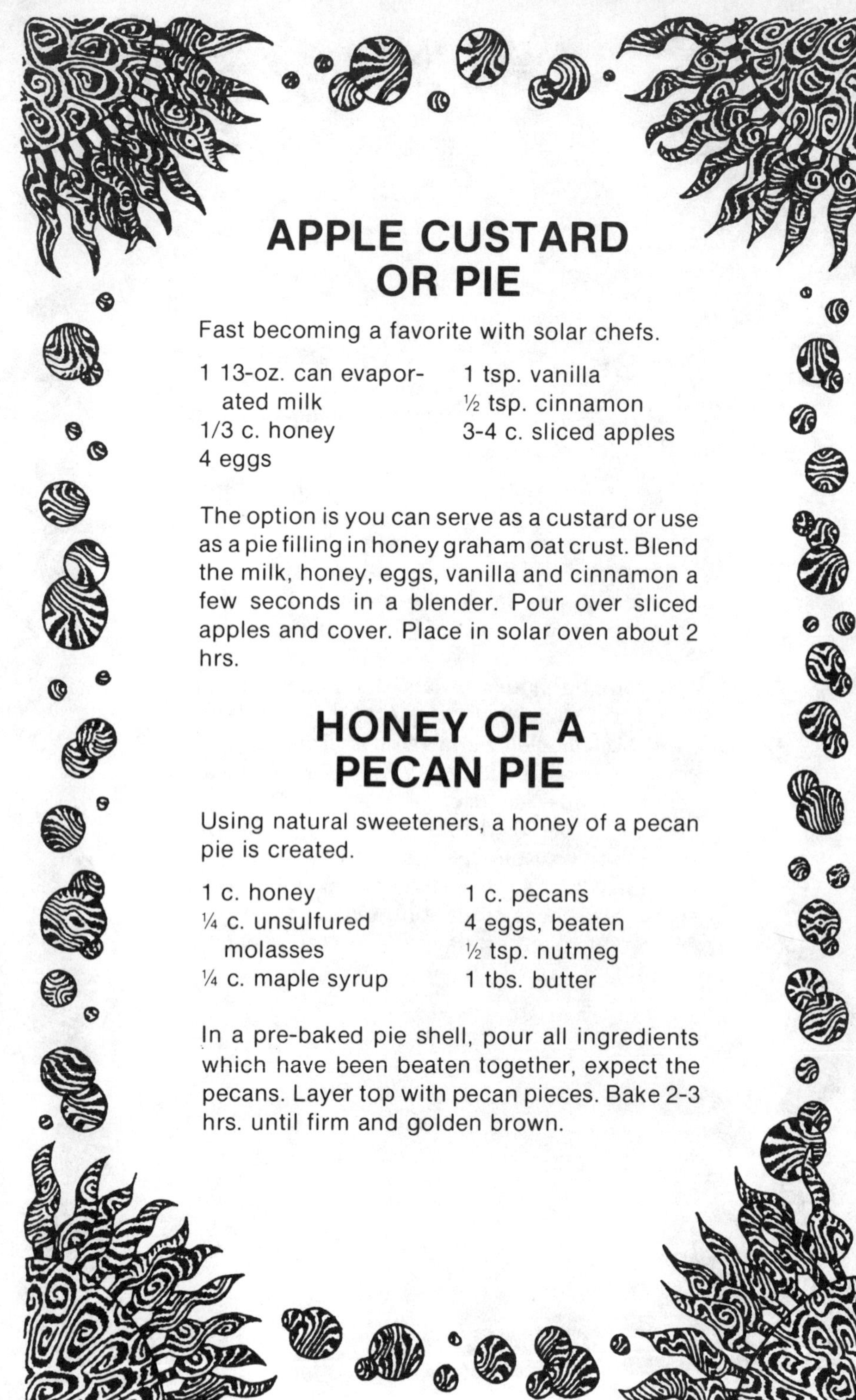

APPLE CUSTARD
OR PIE

Fast becoming a favorite with solar chefs.

1 13-oz. can evapor-
  ated milk
1/3 c. honey
4 eggs

1 tsp. vanilla
½ tsp. cinnamon
3-4 c. sliced apples

The option is you can serve as a custard or use as a pie filling in honey graham oat crust. Blend the milk, honey, eggs, vanilla and cinnamon a few seconds in a blender. Pour over sliced apples and cover. Place in solar oven about 2 hrs.

HONEY OF A
PECAN PIE

Using natural sweeteners, a honey of a pecan pie is created.

1 c. honey
¼ c. unsulfured
  molasses
¼ c. maple syrup

1 c. pecans
4 eggs, beaten
½ tsp. nutmeg
1 tbs. butter

In a pre-baked pie shell, pour all ingredients which have been beaten together, expect the pecans. Layer top with pecan pieces. Bake 2-3 hrs. until firm and golden brown.

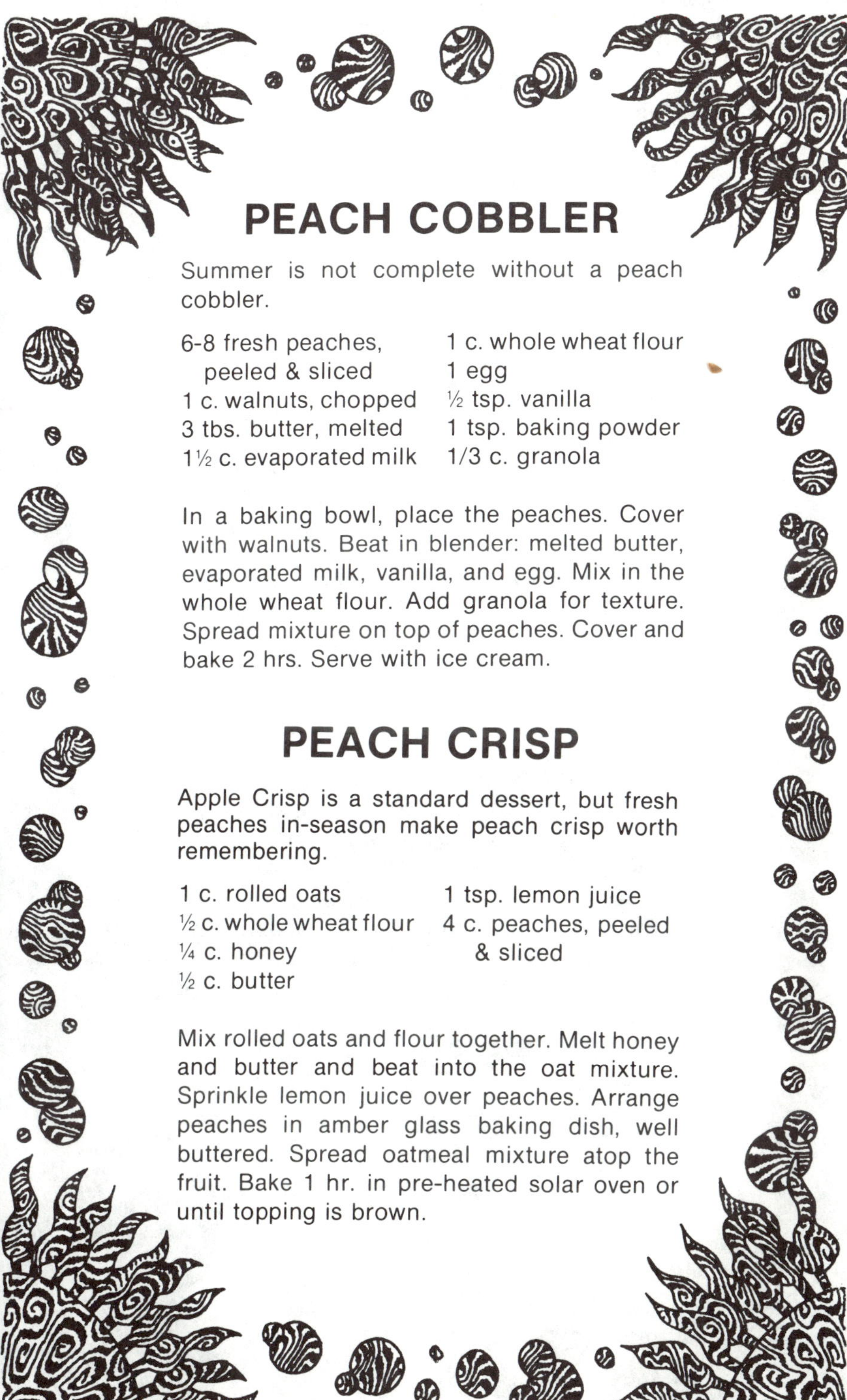

PEACH COBBLER

Summer is not complete without a peach cobbler.

6-8 fresh peaches, peeled & sliced
1 c. walnuts, chopped
3 tbs. butter, melted
1½ c. evaporated milk
1 c. whole wheat flour
1 egg
½ tsp. vanilla
1 tsp. baking powder
1/3 c. granola

In a baking bowl, place the peaches. Cover with walnuts. Beat in blender: melted butter, evaporated milk, vanilla, and egg. Mix in the whole wheat flour. Add granola for texture. Spread mixture on top of peaches. Cover and bake 2 hrs. Serve with ice cream.

PEACH CRISP

Apple Crisp is a standard dessert, but fresh peaches in-season make peach crisp worth remembering.

1 c. rolled oats
½ c. whole wheat flour
¼ c. honey
½ c. butter
1 tsp. lemon juice
4 c. peaches, peeled & sliced

Mix rolled oats and flour together. Melt honey and butter and beat into the oat mixture. Sprinkle lemon juice over peaches. Arrange peaches in amber glass baking dish, well buttered. Spread oatmeal mixture atop the fruit. Bake 1 hr. in pre-heated solar oven or until topping is brown.

MOLASSES COOKIES

Grandmother knew the benefits of molasses (high in natural iron) and she shares her knowledge with good old-fashioned cookies.

4-5 c. whole wheat flour
1 tbs. baking soda
2 tsp. baking powder
1 tsp. ginger
1½ tsp. cinnamon
1 c. butter
1 c. honey
½ c. strong herbal tea (peppermint and ginger is nice)
1 egg, beaten
½ c. molasses

Mix the dry ingredients. Cream the butter, honey and egg. Beat in molasses and warm tea. Add dry ingredients. Mix well. Refrigerate at least 3 hrs. and roll to ¼ inch. Cut as desired. This cookie dough refrigerates up to two days. Make in advance and cook on a sunny day about 45 mins. or more in a pre-heated solar oven.

BIG ISLAND CAKE

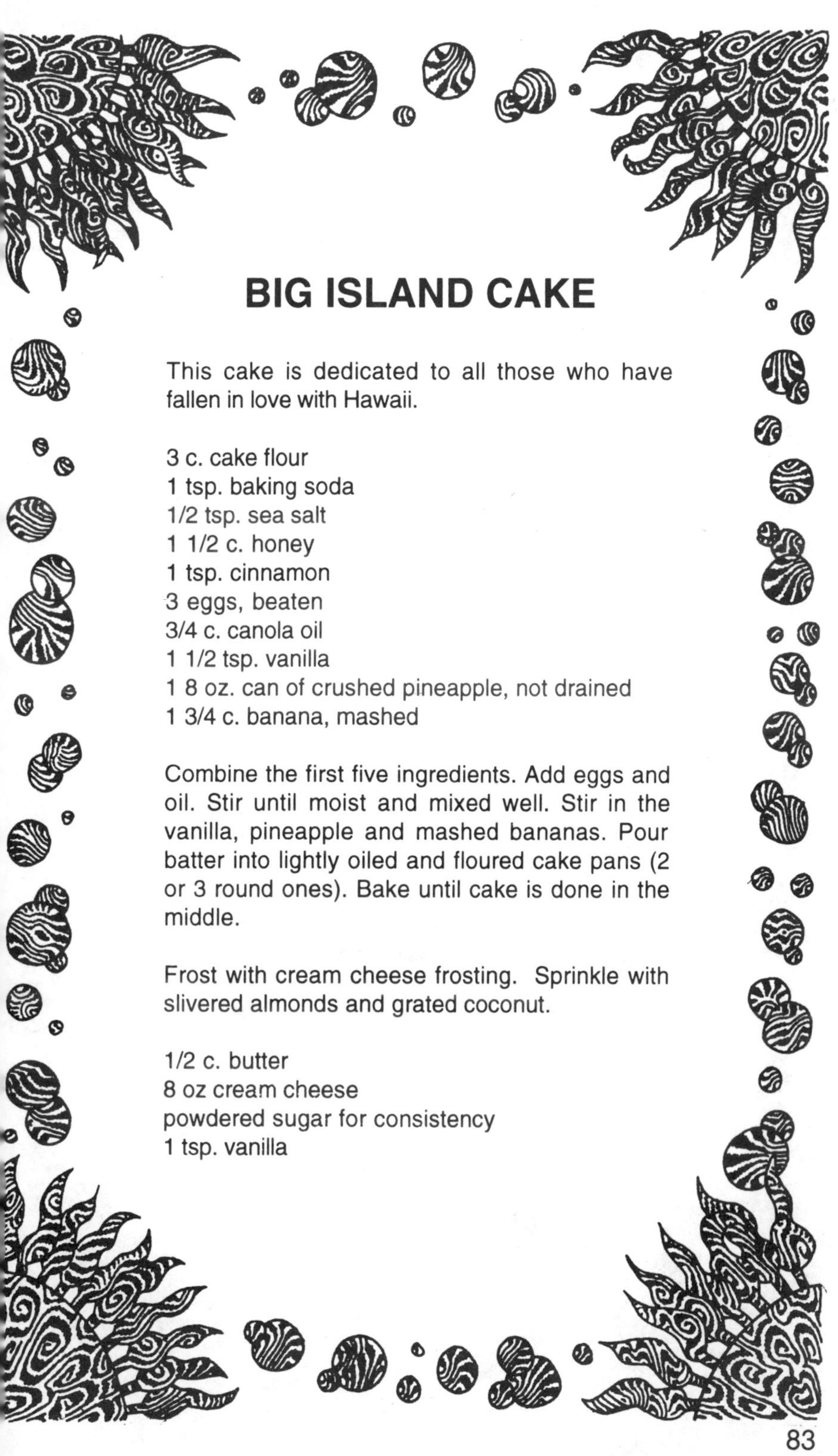

This cake is dedicated to all those who have fallen in love with Hawaii.

3 c. cake flour
1 tsp. baking soda
1/2 tsp. sea salt
1 1/2 c. honey
1 tsp. cinnamon
3 eggs, beaten
3/4 c. canola oil
1 1/2 tsp. vanilla
1 8 oz. can of crushed pineapple, not drained
1 3/4 c. banana, mashed

Combine the first five ingredients. Add eggs and oil. Stir until moist and mixed well. Stir in the vanilla, pineapple and mashed bananas. Pour batter into lightly oiled and floured cake pans (2 or 3 round ones). Bake until cake is done in the middle.

Frost with cream cheese frosting. Sprinkle with slivered almonds and grated coconut.

1/2 c. butter
8 oz cream cheese
powdered sugar for consistency
1 tsp. vanilla

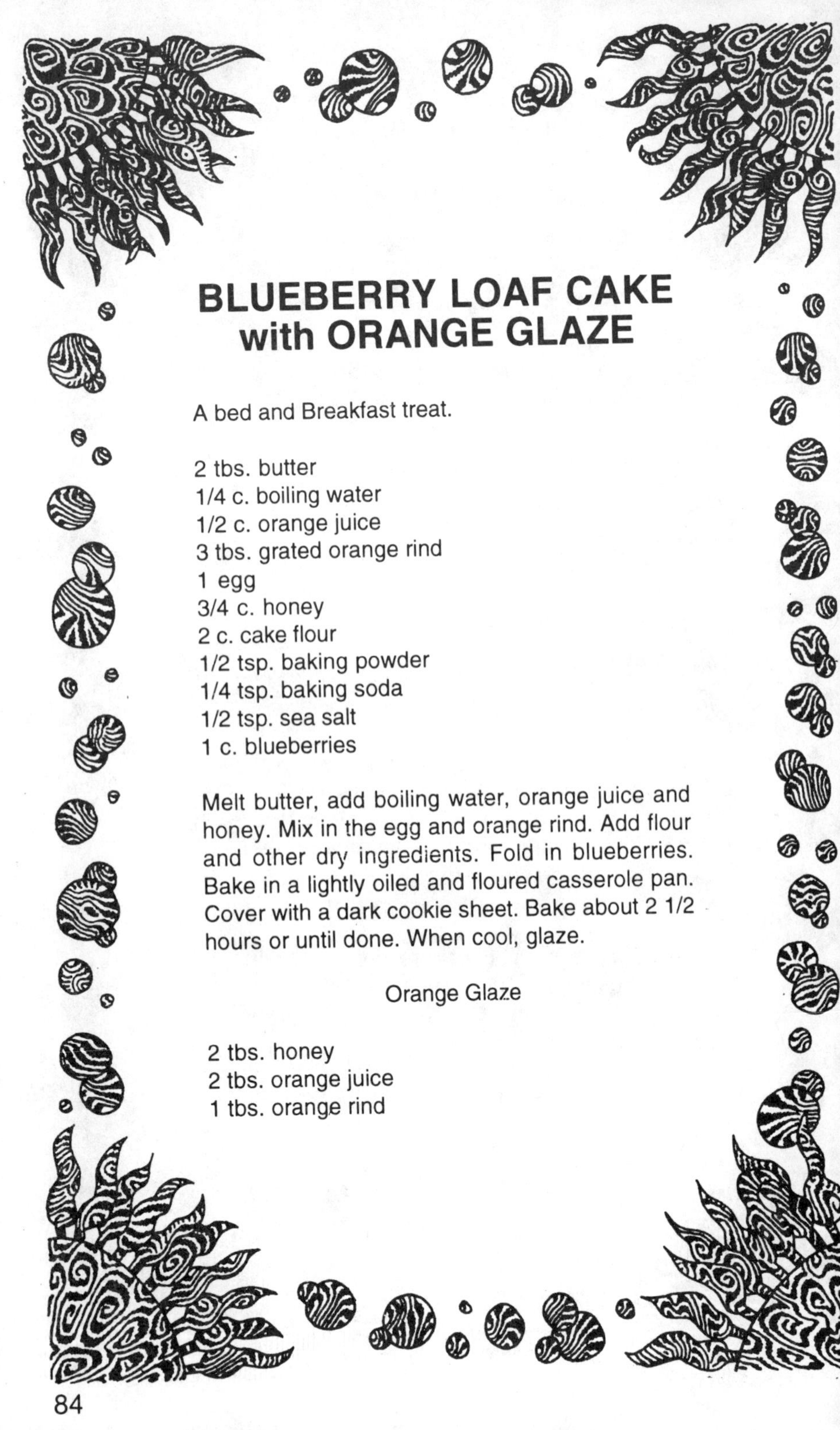

BLUEBERRY LOAF CAKE
with ORANGE GLAZE

A bed and Breakfast treat.

2 tbs. butter
1/4 c. boiling water
1/2 c. orange juice
3 tbs. grated orange rind
1 egg
3/4 c. honey
2 c. cake flour
1/2 tsp. baking powder
1/4 tsp. baking soda
1/2 tsp. sea salt
1 c. blueberries

Melt butter, add boiling water, orange juice and honey. Mix in the egg and orange rind. Add flour and other dry ingredients. Fold in blueberries. Bake in a lightly oiled and floured casserole pan. Cover with a dark cookie sheet. Bake about 2 1/2 hours or until done. When cool, glaze.

Orange Glaze

2 tbs. honey
2 tbs. orange juice
1 tbs. orange rind

CARROT COOKIES

Not so ordinary, these carrot cookies delight sweet toothes with rewarding ingredients.

⅛ tsp. baking soda
½ c. honey
½ c. butter
1 egg, beaten
1 c. whole wheat flour
1 tsp. baking powder
⅛ tsp. sea salt

1 c. quick cooking oats
½ c. wheat germ
½ c. sunflower seeds
½ c. raisins
½ c. grated carrot
1 tsp. vanilla

Stir baking soda into the honey. Cream the butter, beat the egg into it. Add honey mixture. Combine and mix well: flour, baking powder and sea salt. Add to honey butter mixture. Gold *Fold* oats, sunflower seeds, raisins and grated carrots into the dough and add the vanilla. Drop by teaspoon onto black cookie sheets and bake until well browned.

FIG BARS

With local figs in season, fig bars become popular. Substitute dates if figs are unavailable.

1 c. honey
2 eggs
1 c. whole wheat flour

½ c. rolled oats
2 c. fresh figs, peeled
½ c. sunflower seeds

Blend the eggs and honey together. Stir in whole wheat flour, mashed figs, seeds and rolled oats. Pour into an oiled 9 x 13 pan. Bake 2 hrs. and 45 mins. When cool, cut into bars.

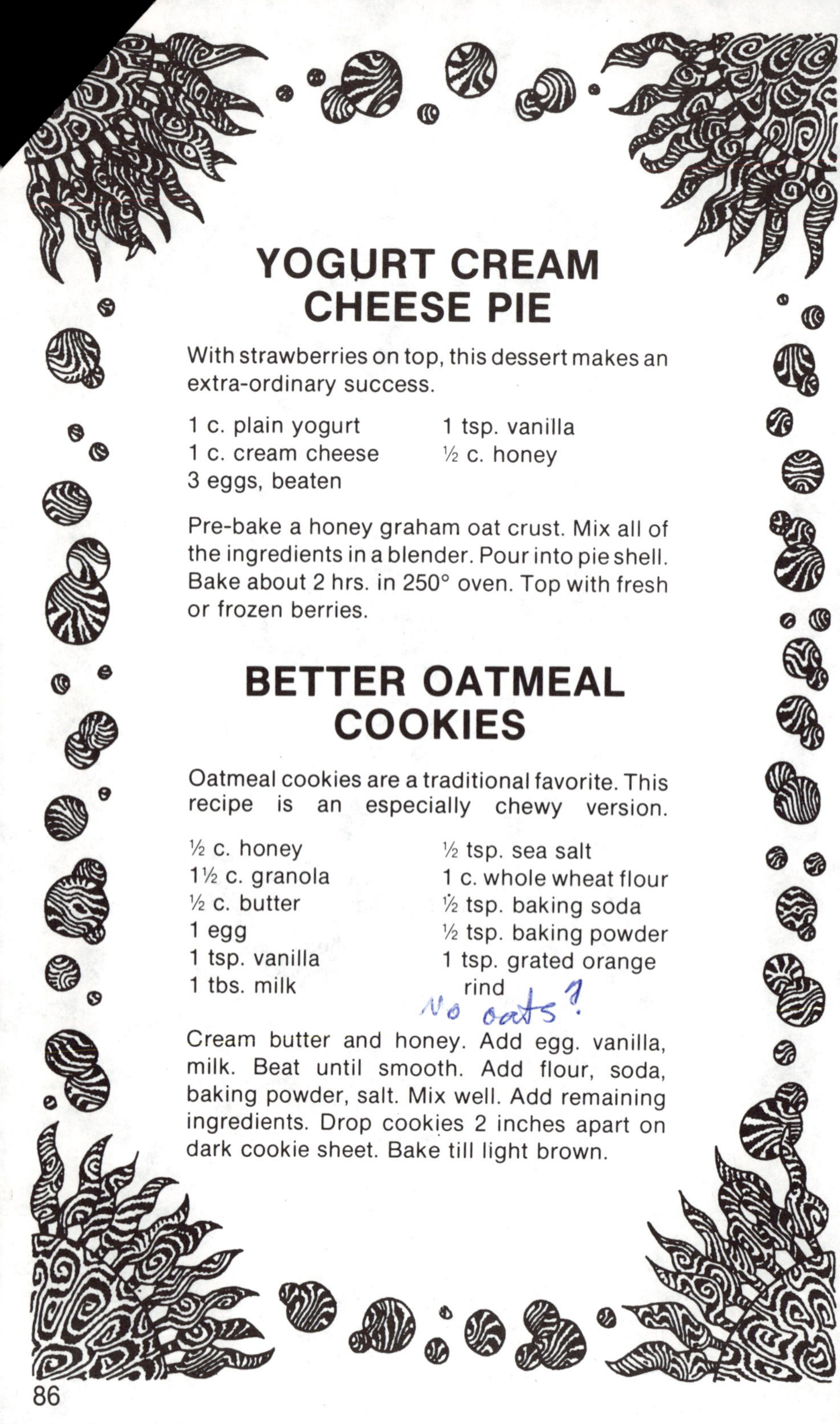

YOGURT CREAM CHEESE PIE

With strawberries on top, this dessert makes an extra-ordinary success.

1 c. plain yogurt
1 c. cream cheese
3 eggs, beaten
1 tsp. vanilla
½ c. honey

Pre-bake a honey graham oat crust. Mix all of the ingredients in a blender. Pour into pie shell. Bake about 2 hrs. in 250° oven. Top with fresh or frozen berries.

BETTER OATMEAL COOKIES

Oatmeal cookies are a traditional favorite. This recipe is an especially chewy version.

½ c. honey
1½ c. granola
½ c. butter
1 egg
1 tsp. vanilla
1 tbs. milk
½ tsp. sea salt
1 c. whole wheat flour
½ tsp. baking soda
½ tsp. baking powder
1 tsp. grated orange rind

Cream butter and honey. Add egg. vanilla, milk. Beat until smooth. Add flour, soda, baking powder, salt. Mix well. Add remaining ingredients. Drop cookies 2 inches apart on dark cookie sheet. Bake till light brown.

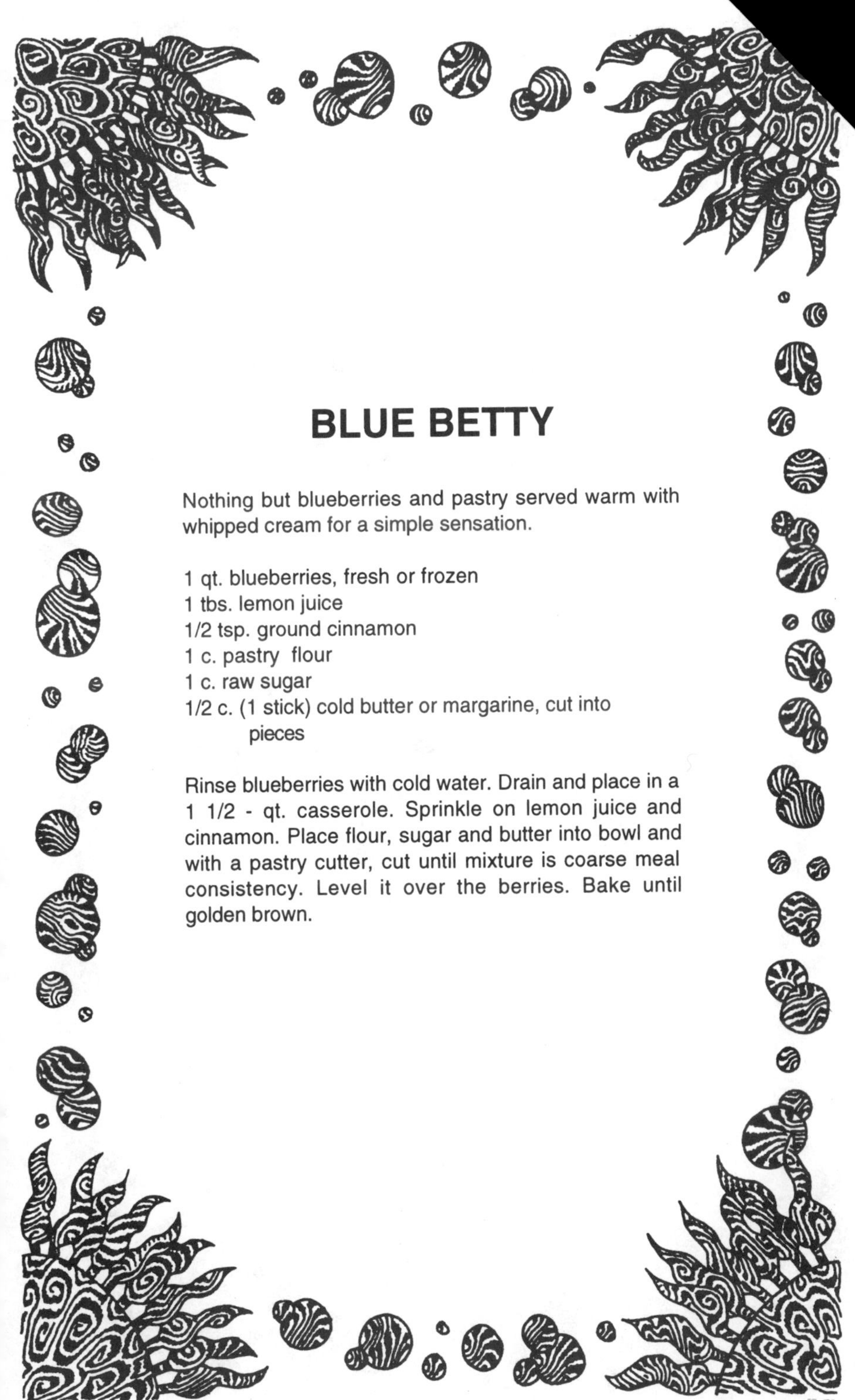

BLUE BETTY

Nothing but blueberries and pastry served warm with whipped cream for a simple sensation.

1 qt. blueberries, fresh or frozen
1 tbs. lemon juice
1/2 tsp. ground cinnamon
1 c. pastry flour
1 c. raw sugar
1/2 c. (1 stick) cold butter or margarine, cut into
       pieces

Rinse blueberries with cold water. Drain and place in a 1 1/2 - qt. casserole. Sprinkle on lemon juice and cinnamon. Place flour, sugar and butter into bowl and with a pastry cutter, cut until mixture is coarse meal consistency. Level it over the berries. Bake until golden brown.

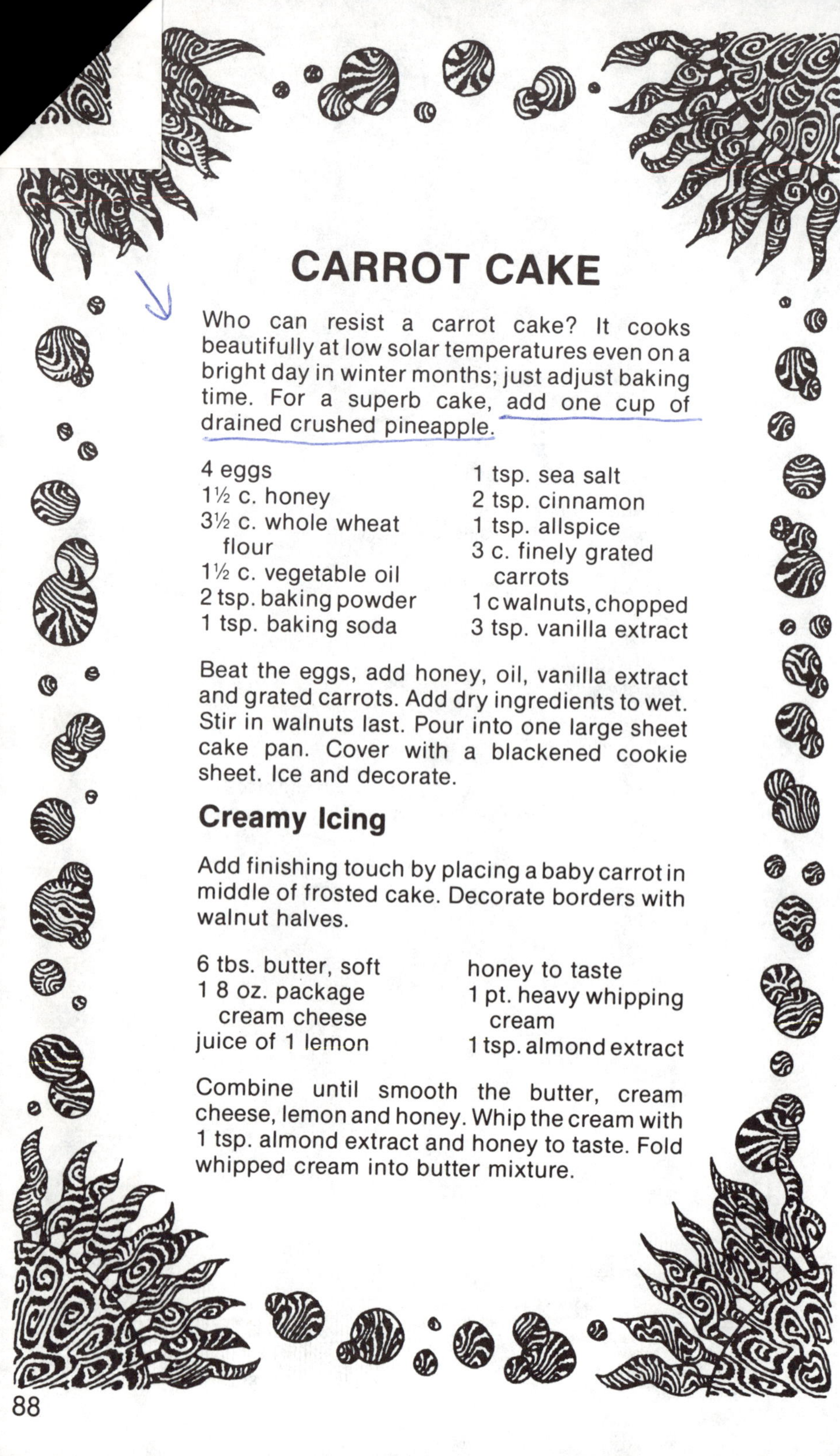

CARROT CAKE

Who can resist a carrot cake? It cooks beautifully at low solar temperatures even on a bright day in winter months; just adjust baking time. For a superb cake, add one cup of drained crushed pineapple.

4 eggs
1½ c. honey
3½ c. whole wheat flour
1½ c. vegetable oil
2 tsp. baking powder
1 tsp. baking soda

1 tsp. sea salt
2 tsp. cinnamon
1 tsp. allspice
3 c. finely grated carrots
1 c walnuts, chopped
3 tsp. vanilla extract

Beat the eggs, add honey, oil, vanilla extract and grated carrots. Add dry ingredients to wet. Stir in walnuts last. Pour into one large sheet cake pan. Cover with a blackened cookie sheet. Ice and decorate.

Creamy Icing

Add finishing touch by placing a baby carrot in middle of frosted cake. Decorate borders with walnut halves.

6 tbs. butter, soft
1 8 oz. package cream cheese
juice of 1 lemon

honey to taste
1 pt. heavy whipping cream
1 tsp. almond extract

Combine until smooth the butter, cream cheese, lemon and honey. Whip the cream with 1 tsp. almond extract and honey to taste. Fold whipped cream into butter mixture.

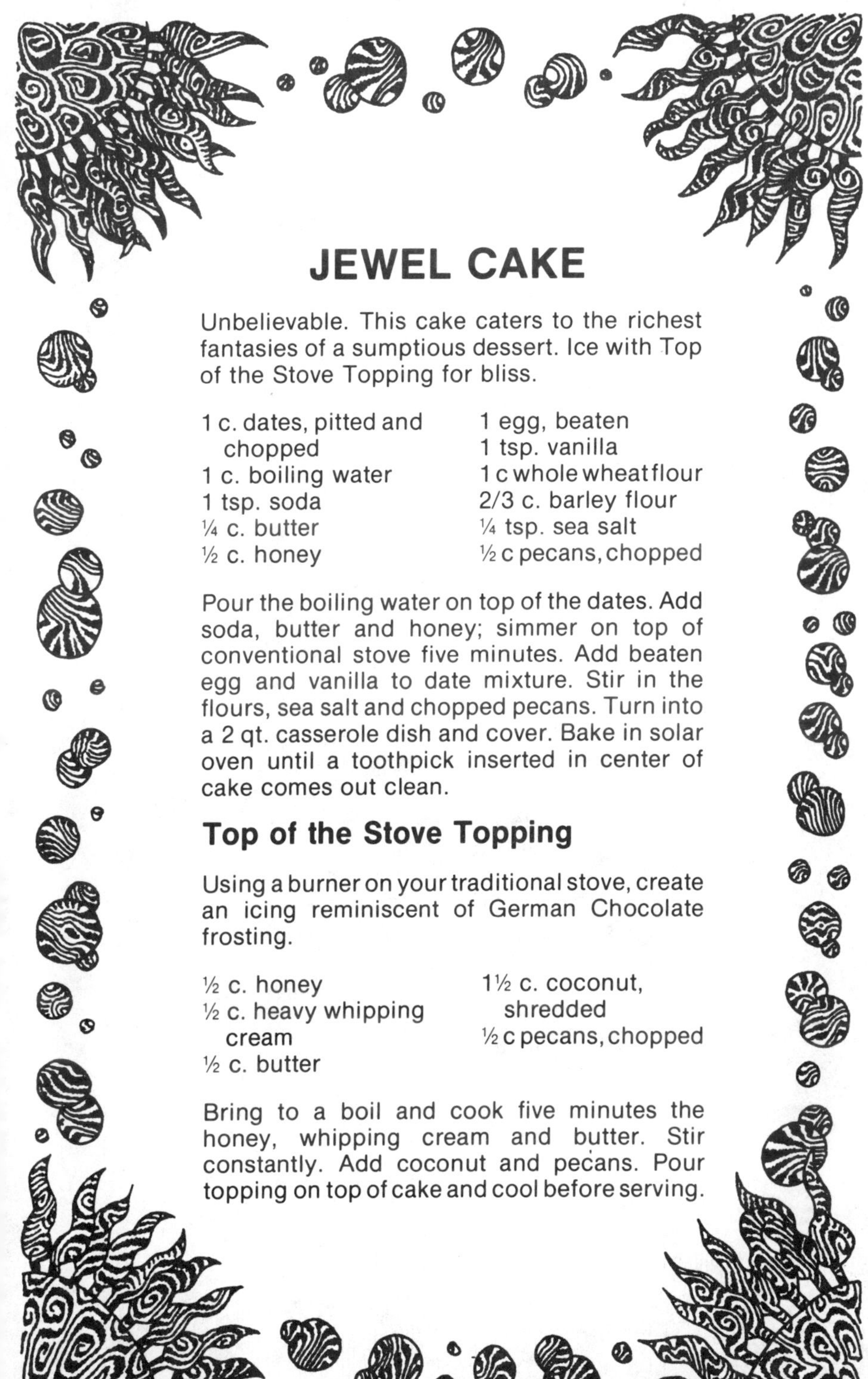

JEWEL CAKE

Unbelievable. This cake caters to the richest fantasies of a sumptious dessert. Ice with Top of the Stove Topping for bliss.

1 c. dates, pitted and chopped
1 c. boiling water
1 tsp. soda
¼ c. butter
½ c. honey

1 egg, beaten
1 tsp. vanilla
1 c whole wheat flour
2/3 c. barley flour
¼ tsp. sea salt
½ c pecans, chopped

Pour the boiling water on top of the dates. Add soda, butter and honey; simmer on top of conventional stove five minutes. Add beaten egg and vanilla to date mixture. Stir in the flours, sea salt and chopped pecans. Turn into a 2 qt. casserole dish and cover. Bake in solar oven until a toothpick inserted in center of cake comes out clean.

Top of the Stove Topping

Using a burner on your traditional stove, create an icing reminiscent of German Chocolate frosting.

½ c. honey
½ c. heavy whipping cream
½ c. butter

1½ c. coconut, shredded
½ c pecans, chopped

Bring to a boil and cook five minutes the honey, whipping cream and butter. Stir constantly. Add coconut and pecans. Pour topping on top of cake and cool before serving.

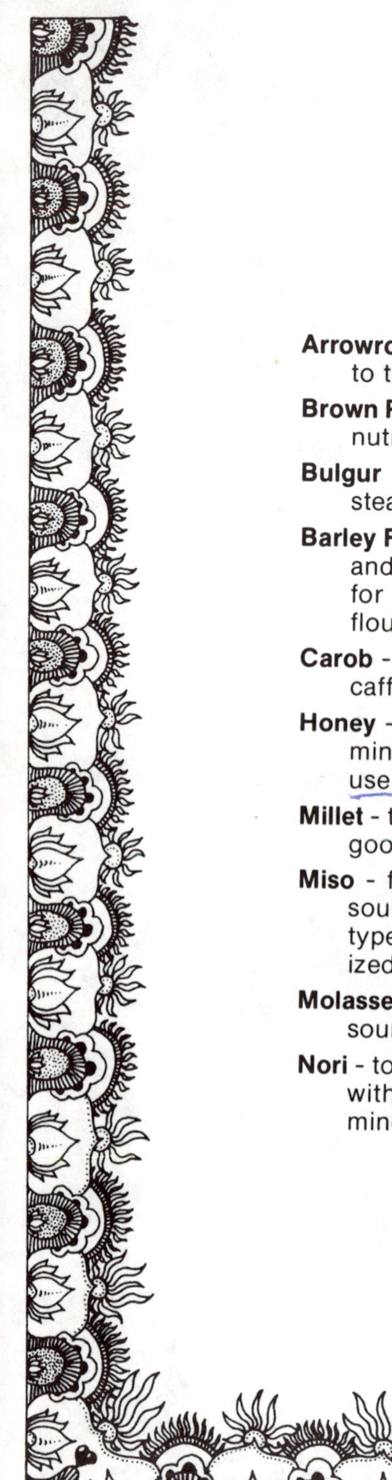

GLOSSARY OF INGREDIENTS

Arrowroot Flour - an easily digested starch to thicken sauces.

Brown Rice - unrefined brown rice contains all nutrients put there by nature.

Bulgur - wheat which has been cracked, steamed and toasted.

Barley Flour - a useful flour containing protein and calcium. One cup may be substituted for a nutritional boost in place of wheat flour.

Carob - a substitute for chocolate that has no caffeine and contains calcium.

Honey - the natural product of bees is high in minerals; for replacing sugar in recipes, use one half the amount of honey.

Millet - the most easily digested of all grains, a good source of low gluten protein.

Miso - fermented soy bean paste which is a source of protein; there are many different types of miso from light to dark, pasteurized and non-pasteurized.

Molasses - unsulfured molasses is a good source of iron.

Nori - toasted, compressed seaweed in sheets with a good source of iodine and sea minerals.